Galen Rowell

The Art of Adventure

Sierra Club Books

SAN FRANCISCO

Library of Congress Cataloging in Publication Data

Rowell, Galen A.
    The art of adventure/Galen Rowell
        p.   cm.
    Captions and essays by Curt Sanburn; edited by David Cohen.
    Originally published: San Francisco: Collins Publishers, 1989.
    ISBN 0-87156-881-0 (pbk.)
    1. Travel photography.   2. Rowell, Galen A.   I. Sanburn, J. Curtis, 1955–   . II.
Cohen David, 1955–   . III. Title.
TR790.R69   1996
770′. 92--dc20   96-8366
                                                                 CIP

Production by Janet Vail
Book and cover design by Mark Ong
Printed in Hong Kong

10 9 8 7 6 5 4 3 2 1

To Barbara, my wife, inspiration and partner in many adventures.

There comes a time—it is the beginning of manhood or womanhood—when one realizes that adventure is as humdrum as routine unless one assimilates it, unless one relates it to a central core which grows within and gives it contour and significance.

Raw experience is empty, just as empty as the forecastle of a whaler, as in the chamber of a counting-house; it is not what one does, but in a manifold sense, what one realizes, that keeps existence from being vain and trivial. Mankind moves about in worlds not realized. Ages hence people may realize more keenly what has happened today than our contemporaries do. It is the artist, the knower, the sayer, who realizes human experience, who takes the raw lump of ore we find in nature, smelts it, refines it, assays it, and stamps it into coins that can pass from hand to hand and make every man who touches them the richer."

—Lewis Mumford

While thumbing through his late father's files, Galen Rowell found this quote, type-written on a yellowed piece of paper. He remembers that his father read it to him when, as a young child, he first evinced an adventurous spirit.

A great traveler, Galen Rowell is also a generous one. He returns from the world's far edges with splendid gifts—frames of film saturated with light and color, faraway places and high adventure. Like the 18th century sketch-artists who accompanied Captain Cook to the South Sea islands, he shows us remote places and peoples with a faculty that transcends mere illustration.

When Galen asked me to write an introduction to this book, I suggested that one of his many famous admirers might do a better job. Unlike Galen, I have no perceptible talent with a camera nor any suggestion of physical courage. Our peculiar mission at Collins Publishers had been to bring together a group of photographers to capture whole countries on film in a single day. During the course of that odyssey, we were privileged to work with some of the world's greatest shooters. Again and again, we were amazed by their sheer talent. Like Galen, they are masters of light, color and composition and what Cartier-Bresson called, "the decisive moment." They make the ordinary extraordinary.

After editing a dozen books and perhaps a million pictures taken by the pre-eminent lensmen of our time, we still wondered: What makes a good photographer great; what genetic quirk or germ of experience forms the piercing eye?

I remember walking across Red Square late one night with Eddie Adams, Pulitzer Prize winner and widely regarded as "the photojournalist's photojournalist." Between furtive glances at our KGB tail, I asked him why some people can see a great picture before it is committed to film and others could not. Eddie, never known as a loquacious man, said he didn't know. Then he casually pointed at the half-moon rising beside a Kremlin tower. The tower was topped with an illuminated red star. It was perfect, just the right moment, and of course, I hadn't see it at all.

So is all of this great photography business unexplainable because we have no lexicon? Is it like one explanation of early childhood—plainly remembered, but unexpressible now because we had no vocabulary then?

There is a case for that. We work with photographs all day long nearly every day, and a lot of what we do involves separating good pictures from bad ones. When we come across a bad picture, we can normally tell you why it is bad, and when we find a good one, we can frequently offer a comment on that, too. But on those very rare

occasions when we find a truly great picture, that one in ten thousand rolls, we are nearly always at a loss for words. Why is this one frame of film so great? We cannot tell you, but we know it is. And we know it as instinctively as we know the Grand Canyon is magnificent or the Taj Mahal sublime.

When we first saw the work of Galen Rowell, we were at a loss for words. The breadth of his experience, the magnitude of his physical courage, his deeply held concern for the environment— these were no match for the ineffable beauty of his pictures. His pictures took your breath away, transported you to far-away places, made you feel like a child again, snuggled in bed, reading *Kon-Tiki.*

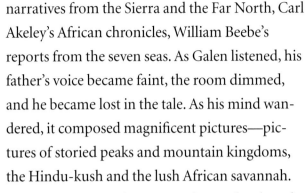

Here also was that *rara avis,* a photographer who could write articulately about his work. A brave adventurer whose mad exploits had decidedly philosophical underpinnings. But when I asked him about his photography, how he made a rectangle of Kodachrome evanescent, why he dangled off thousand-foot cliffs to get "just the right shot," Galen recalled his own boyhood.

Every evening before he went to sleep, Galen's father, a professor of philosophy at Berkeley, would read adventure stories to him: John Muir's narratives from the Sierra and the Far North, Carl Akeley's African chronicles, William Beebe's reports from the seven seas. As Galen listened, his father's voice became faint, the room dimmed, and he became lost in the tale. As his mind wandered, it composed magnificent pictures—pictures of storied peaks and mountain kingdoms, the Hindu-kush and the lush African savannah. Pictures much grander than the grainy little black-and-white illustrations on the page.

When he grew up, Galen went out to find the pictures he had already constructed in his head. And strangely, wonderfully, he did.

In the process, he met challenges of heroic proportions, and not ordinary, run-of-the-mill heroic, either. Galen became the elemental type who conquers mountains and fords dangerous streams, who tries to save the land and the animals, who walks 12 miles down Mt. McKinley though sorely wounded. In short, Galen became the outgrowth of his own imagination—the real-life version of a bold adventurer who usually lives only in the imagination of a 12-year-old boy.

This book of Galen's adventures is illustrated with his camerawork. In some ways, it is a mid-

A Slot Canyon in Arizona Blushes
under a cascade of midday sunlight. Galen
lowered himself on a rope to follow the
light into this voluptuous sandstone
chamber. "The possibilities of integrating
light with landscapes are infinite," Galen
says, "and it is the photographer's task to
choose moments that best express the
meaning of the subject." (1985)

Like a Challenge to the Stormy Sky,
a dead bristlecone pine hugs the earth
high in the windy White Mountains of
eastern California. Bristlecones are the
oldest living things on earth. A live tree
nearby set seed in 2600 B.C. during the
time of the pharaohs. (1988)

Astroman Free-Climb
Yosemite National Park, California, 1985

Ron Kauk is a Yosemite legend. In 1975, at the age of 17, he became the first man to free-climb the Astroman, a 1,400-foot over-hang on the eastern exposure of Washington Column in Yosemite Valley.

The face of Astroman poses a serious challenge to the skills of a free-climber, who must use only his hands and feet (sometimes shoulders, knees, and elbows) to do all the hoisting and holding on. Ropes, pitons, chocks, cams and stoppers are used the way acrobats use safety nets: only in an emergency, to stop a fall.

Ten years after Ron's historic feat, Galen teamed up with him for this dizzying portrait of a rock-jock. At left, Ron sets a *friend,* a cam device used to anchor the safety rope, in a jam crack on Astroman's sheer granite face.

Rock-climbing routes are broken up into pitches determined by the length of the climbing rope and the availability of places to stop. A 1,400-foot route such as Astroman breaks down into 12 pitches with a 165-foot rope.

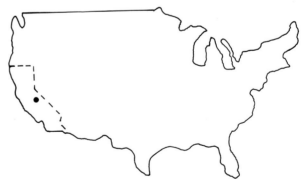

Astroman Free-Climb
Yosemite National Park, California, 1985

The Spiderman Moves and Grooves
of a free-climber. Above: Gymnasts' chalk
increases the friction between skin and
stone. Left: High above Yosemite Valley,
Ron Kauk casually clings to a knobby
handhold. To get this shot, Galen, a world-
class climber in his own right, ascended
on a separate rope just ahead of Ron. He
dangled close to his subject, catching
views only a curious hawk would otherwise see.

Astroman Free-Climb
Yosemite National Park, California, 1985

Olympian While on Astroman,
climbers Ron Kauk and Werner Braun
resume a bohemian existence in the parking lot. The trunk of Werner's Pontiac
holds most of his earthly possessions.

Figures on a Vertical Landscape, 1985
Skip Guerin and, once again, Ron Kauk,
free-climb a rock face at Joshua Tree
National Monument in the California
desert. "To capture that certain moment
when something living is in fine balance
with natural forces is one of the most sat-
isfying aspects of photography."
—Galen Rowell, *Mountain Light*

A Storm Clears over El Capitan in Yosemite, 1973
Preceding pages: "Mist and vapor hold the color and intensity of light far better than any solid object. Landscape artists have traditionally used mist as a vehicle to show off their most extravagant colors. The more visionary their approach, the more mist they include." —Galen Rowell, *Mountain Light*

For a Few Days in February,
if conditions are perfect, the setting sun lights Horsetail Fall against the shadowy East Buttress of El Capitan in Yosemite Valley (left). This rare display bears an uncanny likeness to the old Yosemite Firefall, a spectacular shower of burning embers pushed off Glacier Point by park rangers for the entertainment of tourists. The popular Firefall was stopped by park officials in 1968. Horsetail Fall, however, continues to burn brightly when streamflow, clear skies and the angle of the setting sun conspire. Above: Oak trees on the floor of Yosemite Valley. (1973)

Silhouetted Skiers Glide
across the High Sierra's Kern Plateau on
the John Muir Trail. The 212-mile path,
named for the 19th century naturalist, is
the longest unbroken wilderness trail in
America. Galen and two companions
spent 17 days traversing the entire
Yosemite-to-Mt. Whitney route in the
winter of 1988.

The Yosemite High Country, 1987
According to Galen, who was born and
raised in California, his home state "has
everything I ever wanted to photograph,
more beauty and diversity than any other
mountain landscapes I've ever seen. But,"
he says, "I had to go to the Himalayas, New
Zealand, Africa, Canada and Alaska before
I could say that with any authority."

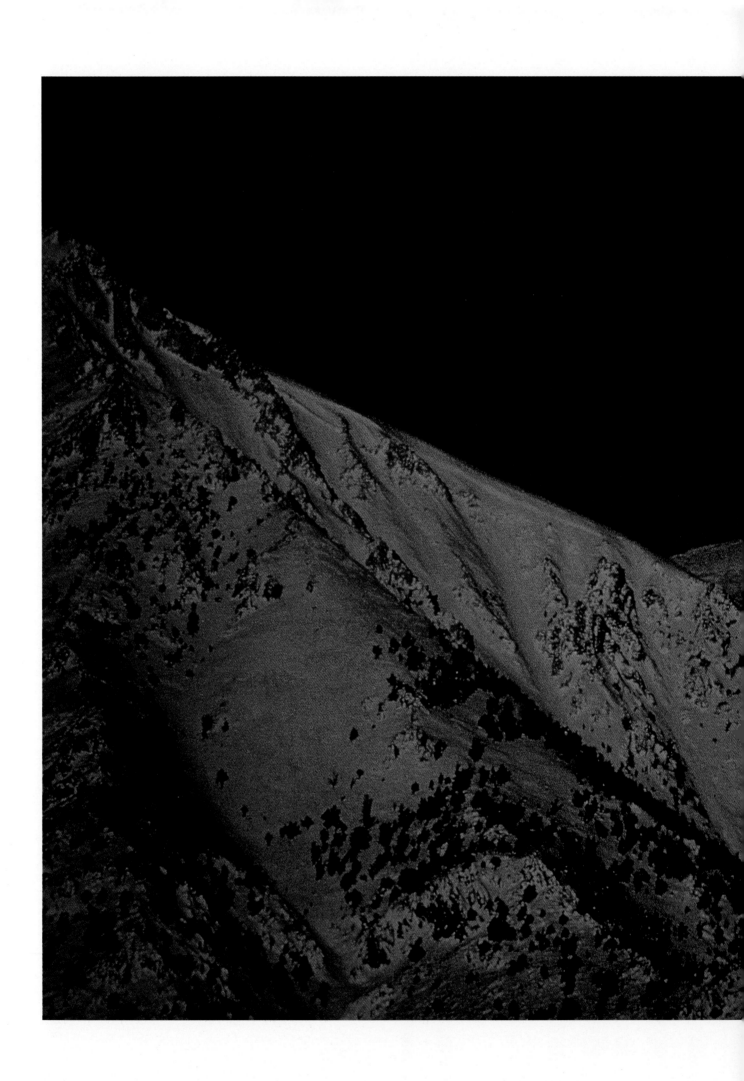

An Unearthly Moonset at Sunrise
over Wheeler Crest. For this picture, Galen
took advantage of "the clearest air I've ever
seen in the eastern Sierra. The red glow of
the sunrise happened right when the setting moon kissed the horizon." (1972)

Monument Valley, Arizona
Following pages: After many trips to this
Navajo tribal park, Galen wanted to avoid
photographic clichés while shooting the
valley's well-known sandstone towers. To
get a new angle, he positioned himself several miles away from his subjects for this
low-lying profile against the eastern sky.
(1986)

The Turquoise of Peyto Lake
in Banff National Park, Alberta, is caused
by the fine silt suspended in glacial runoff.
Galen believes this basin in the Canadian
Rockies is one of the loveliest in the world.
(1982)

Drifting through the Mist,
a small herd of elk gathers near a hot
springs in Yellowstone National Park. Even
in winter, grasses thrive near the park's
steamy springs and geysers. (1978)

Mt. McKinley
Denali National Park, Alaska, 1978

Twenty-thousand-foot Mt. McKinley is the highest peak in North America, and the Kahiltna Glacier is one of five major ice rivers that flow down and around its base. At about 8,000 feet, these glaciers begin to level out and circle the mountain, creating a 90-mile river of ice. Galen Rowell first saw this glacial beltway during a fly-over in 1972.

Six years later, he joined three other adventurers to circumnavigate McKinley on skis, using this route, which no expedition had ever completed. The pioneering three-week trek went relatively smoothly, despite a number of falls, one dislocated shoulder, brittle ice, abrupt storms and more than one unexpected avalanche. On the 19th day of the expedition, the small group discovered faint ski tracks in front of them. It took them a moment to realize that the tracks were their own. They had closed the great circle.

After the expedition, Galen and Ned Gillette, the original planner and leader of the McKinley orbit, decided to try the first one-day ascent of McKinley. The plan was to get up and down the mountain quickly, so they wouldn't need a lot of gear. Speed would also help them avoid high-altitude pulmonary edema, an acute altitude sickness. This kind of climbing, on a mountain like McKinley where expeditions are normally three weeks long, is almost superhuman.

On their first attempt, the snow abruptly turned to blue ice at 13,400 feet. Ned slipped as he was about to switch from skis to crampons. The two men were roped together, and as Ned fell, he popped Galen off the mountain with him. Galen tried to break the fall by jamming his ski pole into

Mt. McKinley
Denali National Park, Alaska, 1978

A Furious Avalanche

off one of McKinley's hanging glaciers interrupts a still morning on Ruth Glacier. With a sudden blast of cold wind, the cloud from the avalanche roared across the narrow valley, engulfing Galen and the rest of the skiers. They were coated with a half-inch of snow that powered through parka seams, zippers and cuffs, down to their polypropylene underwear. Galen snapped this photo before quickly zipping his camera in his hip sack.

Crampons Flashing,

Doug Weins leaps across one of the many crevasses on the Peters Glacier that bedeviled the Mt. McKinley orbit expedition.

Mt. McKinley
Denali National Park, Alaska, 1978

Ice Age Terrain Overwhelms Adventurers on Peters Glacier during the McKinley orbit expedition. The vast glaciers and mind-bending isolation of the Alaska Range later fed Galen's dream of an even more ambitious ski tour through the Karakoram Himalaya.

After Climbing McKinley in One Day, Ned Gillette flies down the mountain on skis he and Galen had stashed, along with Galen's 35mm camera, at 13,000 feet on the way up. Sadly, Galen's photographic record of the summit was lost, permanently shredded in the frozen mechanism of a 6-ounce Minox camera.

Like Yosemite in the Pleistocene,
Ruth Gorge in the Alaska Range is a sheer-walled granite valley. In 1974, Galen made the first ascent of the 5,000-foot southeast face of Mt. Dickey, the highest rock wall in America, visible just right of center in this aerial view. (1986)

Alaska's Transportation of Choice
Galen's wife, Barbara, flies close to the dizzying walls of the upper Ruth Gorge in their Cessna 206 Turbo. Alaska bush pilot Doug Geeting flew Galen into position for this shot. (1986)

On the Backside of Mt. Dickey,
Galen suddenly found himself dangling
from a safety rope 35 feet down a deep,
hidden crevasse. Despite the plummet,
Galen had the presence of mind—and
sense of humor—to snap this picture of
his concerned companion peering into the
hole. (1974)

Don Sheldon's Mountain House
on the ledge of Ruth Gorge is the only
building in thousands of square miles of
icy wilderness in the Alaska Range. (1978)

Every Summer, Alaska's McNeil River hosts a convention of giant Alaskan brown bears that gather to feed on spawning salmon. At one point during this portrait session, Galen counted 31 bears within a hundred yards of his camera. For safety, Galen was accompanied by a fish and game warden carrying a loaded shotgun. (1979)

Reflection Pond, Denali National Park, Alaska
"I had fine light coming in from three different places," Galen says of one of his favorite landscapes, "alpenglow up in the clouds, side-light coming onto the grasses, and the soft light from the sky on the berries and leaves in the foreground." (1986)

A Shinto Shrine, Circa A.D. 703,
tops Mount Tateyama in Japan's Northern
Alps. Galen climbed the peak during the
night to make this image at dawn on June
7, 1985, while working on *A Day in the Life
of Japan.*

Siberia's "Blue Pearl,"
Lake Baikal is the deepest lake in the
world, a natural reservoir for 22 percent of
the earth's fresh water. Galen photographed the crystal waters in southern
Siberia on May 15, 1987, when he joined
100 international photographers to document *A Day in the Life of the Soviet Union.*

The Annapurna Range
rises behind a camp in the Nepal
Himalaya. Following pages: Galen
donated his time to the World Wildlife
Fund to document the creation of the
Annapurna Conservation Area, a model
for future nature preserves in the Third
World. (1987)

Visible from Outer Space,

the 1,500-mile Great Wall of China was completed in A.D. 221. More than 300,000 men took ten years to complete the barricade. Galen first encountered the Great Wall in 1980, and returned three years later to make this winter image on his way to Mt. Everest.

The Ancient Kingdom of Baltistan,

now part of Pakistan, was founded where sands and snows meet in the heights of Central Asia. Here, three members of a Balti family cross the Skardu Valley on their way to market. Behind them lie the foothills of the Karakoram Himalaya. (1984)

slowed to four miles a day. On these days, time and distance became glacial.

Forty-four days after stepping onto the Siachen Glacier, the expeditioners ended their trek at Hunza, having traversed most of Pakistan, east to west from the Indian border almost to Afghanistan. Right: An aerial view of Biafo Glacier, the third leg of the Karakoram traverse.

The adventurers' re-entry to civilization was muted. The trauma of moving through the Karakoram, day after day under their own power, had numbed them and drained the color from the experience. Their capacity for emotional response had shrunk to near zero. It was not until months later that Galen felt full satisfaction from the most unprecedented adventure of his life.

The Karakoram Ski Traverse
Pakistan, Winter, 1980

Camp on the Siachen Glacier

near the starting point of the Karakoram traverse. From Galen's journal: "There is little conversation today. We wait for the sun to warm us so we can break camp. I wonder if my friends share the fears that kept me awake in the hours before dawn."

A Portrait of Kim Schmitz,

Galen's tentmate, on a minus-25 degree morning during the Karakoram traverse. A veteran of six Himalayan expeditions with Galen, Kim's strength is legendary among mountaineers. One sports writer called the steel-eyed climber a cross between Captain Marvel and Conan the Barbarian.

The Karakoram Ski Traverse
Pakistan, Winter, 1980

"The Days Merge into One Another,"
Galen wrote in his journal. During the 285-mile traverse, the four skiers split into two teams. The members of each team were roped together in case a hidden crevasse took one of the skiers (left).

Three Men Completed the Traverse
Dan Asay developed knee trouble and left the group midway from the village of Askole. For Kim, Ned and Galen, the foot of the Hispar Glacier marked the end of the ski-traverse, where this photo was made with a self-timer, although several days of trekking to Hunza remained.

The Highest War in History

began when Indian troops suddenly occupied the Pakistani-controlled, uninhabited Siachen Glacier. In 1986, while on assignment for *National Geographic*, Galen was invited by the late President Mohammed Zia-ul-Haq of Pakistan to become the first western journalist to enter the war zone. He traveled by helicopter to camps at altitudes up to 20,500 feet. Right: Pakistani army troops brandish a Chinese-made anti-aircraft gun.

An Unnamed 20,000-Foot Peak

in the Karakoram Himalaya serves as a near-vertical horizon for a retiring crescent moon. To get this shot, Galen used a 500mm lens, underexposed the film to prevent blurring by the movement of the moon and made a lightened duplicate transparency to bring out the detail. "My secret Kodachrome 400," Galen says with a grin. (1975)

"Mother Goddess of Earth,"

Chomolungma is the Tibetan name for Mt. Everest, the world's highest point at 29,028 feet. Galen was the climbing leader of a 1983 expedition whose goal was the first ascent of Everest's West Ridge from the Tibetan side. (1983)

The Valley of the Flowers

another name for the Kama Valley, has
already been damaged by wholesale logging. Still, every spring more than 30
species of rhododendron, each with a
slightly different flower, splash the valley
with rare Himalayan color. (1988)

**Tibetan Women Carry 100-Pound
Timbers**

out of the Kama Valley on the east side of
Mount Everest. It's a three-day trek across
a 16,000-foot pass to the village of Kharta,
where trucks pick up the wood for ship-
ment to the treeless plains of central Tibet.
Deforestation, long a serious problem in
the lush Himalayan valleys of Nepal, is
even more serious in arid Tibet where forest cover is rare. Increasing demand for
lumber and firewood, agricultural expan-
sion and improved road access to the
remote forests are making matters worse.
Galen was the first journalist to report this
story, for *National Geographic Magazine* in
1988.

Swayambu Temple in Kathmandu
In 1982, Galen and Barbara Rowell traveled with actor Robert Redford through Nepal. The trip included a trek to Everest, a journey on elephants through the jungle and this morning walk through Kathmandu to Swayambu Temple. Left: The temple emerges from valley fog at dawn while Buddhist lamas circumambulate the sacred spot.

Kailas and Manasarovar Pilgrimage
Western Tibet, 1987

"The perpetual snow-clad peak of the Holy Kailas, of hoary antiquity and celebrity, the spotless designs of Nature's art, of most bewitching and overpowering beauty, has a vibration of the supreme order . . . It seems to stand as an immediate revelation of the Almighty in concrete form, which makes man bend his knees and lower his head in reverence."
—*Swami Pranavananda, 1949*

For Tibetan Buddhists and Hindus, Mount Kailas is the center of the universe—the holiest mountain on earth and the snowy parent of the four great rivers, the Brahmaputra, Indus, Karnali and Sutlej. Pilgrims travel thousands of miles to walk the 32-mile holy circle around Kailas.

At 3:00 a.m. on an August morning, Galen Rowell and three Tibetan friends began a one-day holy circle, or *kora,* around the base of Kailas. Hours later, the sacred peak suddenly revealed itself, lit by waning moonlight and a predawn glow in the east. The Tibetans bowed to the ground. Galen found himself doing likewise. Visualizing the peak as the center of the universe inspired him to make a five-minute time-exposure of the moonlit peak beneath a great arc of stars.

One *kora* around Kailas cleanses the sins of one life; after 108, the pilgrim achieves nirvana. For the supremely pious, there is the grueling *sashtanga-danda-pradakshina,* a holy circle executed in a continuous series of bodily prostrations so that the length of the body itself draws the circle around Kailas. The 22,000-foot mountain remains sacred and unclimbed by modern mountaineers. Tibetan Buddhists, however, tell

the story of a beloved 11th century saint, Milarepa, who ascended to the summit on a beam of light.

Nearby, Lake Manasarovar (left) is considered the first and holiest lake, worshipped even before the dawn of history. Together with Kailas, Manasarovar is the most important Himalayan place of pilgrimage. According to Swami Pranavananda, the spiritual vibrations emanating from the austere landscape "soothe and lull even the most wandering mind into sublime serenity and transport it into involuntary ecstasies." An entry in Galen's journal recounts his arrival at Kailas: "Near the pass, the land grew ever more austere … we seemed to be riding on the bones of the earth, elevated above the soft body of the world. It was easy to understand how pilgrims, walking overland for weeks or months, felt they were approaching the center of the universe."

Kailas and Manasarovar Pilgrimage
Western Tibet, 1987

Kailas Pilgrims Shed Old Clothes
and possessions as they circle the mountain (left). Abandoning material goods complements the spiritual cleansing of the journey. Among the clothing, jewelry and shoes, Galen found a mummified head and other body parts, the remains of the sick and elderly who came to die at Kailas. Above: The bodies of the dead are often cut into pieces for a celestial burial so that Tibetan vultures, such as this lammergeier, will carry the pieces to heaven.

Kailas and Manasarovar Pilgrimage
Western Tibet, 1987

Tsewang Tsambu Traveled 500 Miles
on foot across the Tibetan Plateau to make
the Kailas *kora*. On the way, he met Galen
and his Tibetan-speaking traveling companions who drove him to Kailas in their
truck. Tsewang circled the holy mountain
and washed away the sins of this life, as
Galen did. Galen would meet Tsewang
again a year later, in a faraway region of
Tibet.

Like a Scene out of *Casablanca,*
a Russian-built Chinese airliner waits out
the early-morning fog at Chengdu airport.
Runway lights silhouette four members of
Galen's 1983 Everest expedition en route
to Lhasa, Tibet.

The View from the Lhasa Hotel
with Potala Palace barely visible in the
background. Galen laments the sterile new
Chinese architecture in the middle of this
ancient holy city and lists other surprising
intrusions on the adventurer's dreams of
Lhasa: ubiquitous Chinese soldiers, traffic
cops, billboards and even a place called the
Lhasa Disco. (1988)

A Kirghiz Father and Son

crossed paths with the peripatetic photographer twice: in 1980 and then again in 1986. The first time, Galen was en route to Muztagata in Xinjiang province, China. The portrait below was published in his book *Mountains of the Middle Kingdom.* Six years later, he returned to the area. He showed the book to a man who took one look at the portrait and rushed into a nearby building. Out came the same Kirghiz father and son—and their entire family—to greet Galen, and once again pose for his camera.

A Uygur Family Harvests Wheat
on a communal farm near Kashgar.
Uygurs (pronounced wee-gurs) are a
Moslem minority group in western China.
The region used to be called Turkestan
because so many of its inhabitants were of
Turkish descent. (1986)

A Passage to Africa

is *de rigueur* for any world adventurer, and, in 1982, Galen and his wife, Barbara, set out for Tanzania and Kenya. Left: In Masai Mara Reserve they found three young lions roughhousing. Below: In Tanzania's Ngorongoro Crater they found some even younger cubs lounging on the rocks.

Acacia Trees, Tanzania

Preceding pages: Using a 600mm lens, perfectly clear air, the canopy of an acacia tree—and no filter—Galen records an African dawn on the Serengeti Plain. (1982)

Life and Death on the African Plain
A scavenged cape buffalo carcass evokes the primeval feeling of the grassy Ngorongoro plains. Right: A bull elephant bluff-charges Galen's Land Rover at Samburu Game Reserve in northern Kenya. (1982)

Wary Flamingos
at Ngorongoro Crater shift about nervously to keep a safe distance while a spotted hyena pretends he's out for an evening stroll (following pages). (1982)

On the Plains of Patagonia,
a storybook peak called Fitz Roy rises
10,000 feet above a herd of wild horses
(preceding pages). Patagonia straddles
Chile and Argentina at the southern,
windswept tip of South America. Like the
Karakoram Himalaya, many of the peaks
of the Fitz Roy Range are sheer granite
towers draped with ice. Forbidding and
given to vicious weather, Patagonia has
enticed adventurers for years. Butch Cas-
sidy hid out here, and Charles Darwin
gathered evidence for his theory of evolu-
tion. Fitz Roy is named in honor of the
captain of the H.M.S. Beagle which
brought Darwin to Patagonia during a
four-year scientific journey around the
world. Above: Storm clouds light up at
sunrise above Lago Viedma south of Fitz
Roy. (1985) Left: Snowy patches on a
Patagonian peak reflect the alpenglow
from a thundercloud.

Fitz Roy Expedition
Patagonia, Argentina, 1985

They tried to make it in only a day, but darkness beat the climbers to the top of Fitz Roy by a few hundred feet. With no tents or sleeping bags, and scarcely room to stand on an ice ledge, Galen Rowell, Michael Graber and David Wilson were forced to stay up all night. They jogged in place to keep warm on their perilous perch as they waited for dawn's first light. The merest breeze chilled them to the bone but their spirits were high: They were close to the top. They sang songs to keep from shivering.

"Tonight we will have no sleep, no warmth, no food, and no liquid," Galen wrote. "We are lacking those basic aspects of human existence, yet we have come to this by our own choosing; for us it is a privilege to stand the night away near Fitz Roy's summit in clarity and stillness." With first light, the three tired and cold climbers began to move to the top. Within minutes they were there, warmed by their effort and the sun's first rays.

Galen's view from the summit at dawn. From here, they overlooked the sheer spire of Cerro Torre where legendary Italian mountaineer Toni Egger disappeared in an icy storm in 1959. To the west, they could see the arctic expanse of the Patagonian Icecap stretch for 200 miles.

"The power of the view from Fitz Roy," Galen wrote, "comes from within us. It would not be the same from an airplane, or if we had ridden to the summit in a gondola. Thought and vision are intertwined . . . we feel a strong connection between what is before our eyes and the knowledge of our inner selves that we have gained by pushing the outer limits of our endurance."

Fitz Roy Expedition
Patagonia, Argentina, 1985

The Assault on Fitz Roy

Above: Just before nightfall, the winds are blessedly light as David Wilson follows Galen up a sheer wall high on the peak. Fitz Roy is in the path of the legendary Roaring Forties, where fierce atmospheric currents circle the globe's subantarctic latitudes, and blast the Patagonian peaks with hurricane-force winds. Still, late-winter snow and thick ice clog most of the usable cracks and ledges, slowing progress and forcing them to spend the night on an icy ledge. Left: The 2,500-foot final headwall on Fitz Roy looms above Michael Graber as he leads the party along a corniced ridge.

Buttermilk Road, Eastern Sierra, California; 1971

The night before I took this photograph, I drove up Buttermilk Road and slept beside my car. When I awoke to clouds, I was disappointed. I had hoped to photograph the pink flush of alpenglow on the peaks. After the first light failed, I drove off without having taken a single photograph. A mile up the dusty road, a beam of golden sunlight broke onto the desert floor and my first urge was to focus on the foreground rocks before the light disappeared. Instead, I included the blue-shadowed peaks plus the road to lead the viewer's eye through the scene. Here was a perfect opportunity to use edges of natural light to match edges of the natural world and emphasize their meaning. The weather had reversed the normal position of red light on the peaks with blue shadows below into a greater visual truth: warm light touched the warm desert while cool light chilled the snowy peaks above. I braced my camera on the roof of my car and got off three frames before the light was gone.

Nikkormat FTN, 105mm lens, Kodachrome II (ISO 25)

Alpenglow on Keeler Needle (14,240 feet), High Sierra, California; 1976

While camping at 12,000 feet beneath this spire to attempt the first free climb of the 1,800-foot east face with two companions, I got up well before sunrise to photograph first light on the peaks of the eastern escarpment. After I made an often-published broader view of the Mount Whitney massif and all its satellite spires, I singled out Keeler Needle with a short telephoto lens at the height of the rich dawn colors. I wasn't carrying a tripod with all my climbing and camping gear, so I braced my camera on a rock to get as sharp an image as possible. In this view the top of the spire has an eerie, darkened look created by the shadow of a cloud layer that closed in within minutes and prevented us from doing our climb. Three weeks later, we returned in clear weather and succeeded.

Nikkormat FTN, 105mm lens, Kodachrome II (ISO 25)

Moonrise from the summit of Mount Whitney, California; 1987

While shooting what goes on around Labor Day on Mount Whitney for *Sports Illustrated,* I camped on the summit and made this photograph of other hikers watching the moonrise. After shooting the full moon on the horizon in glowing red sunset light, I waited for the more subtle light of the twilight wedge, a boundary of pink and blue light caused by the rising shadow of the earth. The wedge is at its best when seen from high altitude, where the translucent planes of atmosphere lit pink by the sun and blue by the twilight are more closely aligned to one's line of sight than at sea level, where the wedge can be seen on clear nights, but with a much more diffuse boundary. I used a two-stop graduated neutral-density filter to equalize the exposure on the brighter pink light with the shadowed scene below.

Nikon F3, 85mm lens, Fujichrome Professional 50

Rainbow and nesting California gulls, Negit Island, Mono Lake, California; 1974

While covering the Owens Valley of eastern California for the *National Geographic* in 1973 and 1974, I photographed Mono Lake and proposed a separate story on it. I spent the night on Negit Island to catch this scene as evening light created a rainbow after a thunderstorm. My proposal was turned down, both because it would be too soon after a story on the adjoining region and the belief that the issue of the city of Los Angeles depleting the lake's level did not have enough national significance. I later wrote the first national magazine story on Mono Lake for *Audubon,* but it appeared without any photographs because of internal scheduling problems. Thus this photograph celebrating the glory of the island's active nesting colony in the early seventies wasn't published until after Negit ceased to be an island due to the lowering of the lake level in the late seventies. The largest single California gull rookery was thus destroyed when predators gained access. In recent years the colony has begun to recover as the lake's level has increased after public outcry and legal action against Los Angeles.

Nikon FTN, 24mm lens, Kodachrome II (ISO 25)

Vermilion Lakes, Canadian Rockies; 1980

In midwinter I was surprised to find that liquid water had created a mirror surface on this frozen lake in Banff National Park. A combination of warm springs at the edge of the lake and a warm chinook wind had allowed the water to flow in broad arcs across the ice. I didn't shoot any pictures when I first found the scene because the light was flat under cloudy skies. A few days later, however, I saw the full moon low in the sky with the first flush of alpenglow hitting spectacular clouds. I rushed back to the lake in my rental car and quickly set my camera up on a tripod to make this photograph. My meter indicated that the reflection on the lake in deep shadow was a full three stops darker than the sunlit clouds, so I used a two-stop graduated neutral-density filter to open up the shadows and bring the exposure within the film's range. The great light was gone in less than five minutes.

Nikon FM, 55mm lens, Kodachrome 25

Antelope Canyon, near Page, Arizona; 1985

When I descended into this narrow slot canyon, I found myself all alone in a bizarre world of sandstone and light. I had followed instructions from a friend, driven into the back of a trailer park on a Navajo reservation, and walked into a slightly depressed dry wash that quickly became a deep gash in solid rock. I scrambled most of the way, but used an old fixed rope to descend the final 10 feet to the canyon floor with a tripod, a single camera, and a 20mm ultra wide-angle lens. In the decade since then, crowds and closures have affected this site. I feel lucky to have had it all to myself for several hours, choosing angles low to the ground with midday light bouncing off the walls and producing a range of wild reddish tones. At other times of day, or when it is cloudy, the light show is shut off and the sandstone is reduced to a single soft hue.

Nikon F3, 20mm lens, Fujichrome Professional 50

Bristlecone pine and evening storm, White Mountains, California; 1988

I saw the potential for this image while working on a video for Kodak at 11,000 feet in this desert range near the Nevada border. I was supposed to be walking along a ridge crest with bristlecone pines, musing about the great quality of light at sunset. I had asked permission beforehand to take off and shoot a picture when the sun was a minute above the horizon. With a 16mm semi-fisheye lens already on my camera, I plunged down a rocky slope to where I had conceived this image hours earlier. With my camera braced on the ground looking up at the sky through the tree, I framed a more distant tree between the main limbs of this one in the last moments of alpenglow.

Nikon F3, 16mm lens, Kodachrome 25 Professional

Aspen grove below Lake Sabrina, Eastern Sierra, California; 1974

While working on a *National Geographic* story on the Owens Valley, I came across the most beautiful aspen glade I had ever seen, where tall grasses swirled around white trunks with a centerpiece of fresh granite. I shot several rolls of various interpretations and returned several times hoping to take more images in richer fall colors. The grasses were never as verdant, and I came to learn why. A leak in a dam had been repaired and underground seepage no longer gave the glade its unusual quality. The clean granite boulders were the result of blasting for the dam.

Nikon FTN, 24mm lens, Kodachrome II (ISO 25)

Mount Dana at dawn over Mono Lake, California; 1988

On a spring morning at Mono Lake I watched the alpenglow hit 13,053-foot Mount Dana on the border of Yosemite National Park. As the light crept down the slope, I was reminded of the vast Pleistocene glacier that came down Lee Vining Canyon from Mount Dana and spilled icebergs into a very different and far larger Mono Lake. I waited for the light to spill onto the distant row of tufa towers formed by alkaline salts in the lake and got my favorite image when it just touched the edge of the nearest tufa, creating a strong diagonal of bright orange rocks that lead the viewer's eye up to the peak.

Nikon F3, 85mm lens, Fujichrome Professional 50

Ron Kauk leading a crack on Astroman, Yosemite Valley, California; 1985

I was neither a direct participant in Ron's climb nor a remote observer. Ron and I were members of separate climbing teams on the same face on the same day. To get coverage for *Sports Illustrated,* I climbed just ahead of Ron, roped to Werner Braun. When I would find a good camera position, I would ask Werner to tie me off and hold me there to wait for Ron to climb up into my frame. After I got the shot, I had to be careful not to knock him off the rock as I swung over and continued climbing myself. Part of Ron's goal was to counter the prevailing image of the public that unroped free-solo climbing was on the cutting edge of the sport, as depicted in photographs published in *People, Life,* and *Newsweek.* He and I agreed that such photos only serve to confirm the public's preconception that climbers are crazy. Since any climber can always do harder climbing high above the ground with the security of a safety rope, the cutting edge of the sport continues to involve roped climbing.

Nikon F3, 20mm lens, Fujichrome Professional 100

Ron Kauk near the top of Astroman, Yosemite Valley, California; 1985

High above the Yosemite Valley floor, Ron feels perfectly at home with his hands on a flake of granite and his feet braced against a small crack. His safety rope has just been clipped to a cam nut he placed in the crack beneath the flake. Far below, his partner, Dr. Andrew Embick of Valdez, Alaska, is holding the rope and feeding it out through a belaying device that could stop Ron's fall within inches of his present position. As Ron climbs upward, the fall he risks is double the distance to his last safety device, assuming that it holds. With stretchy nylon rope and few ledges on the overhanging cliff, even a fall of 50 feet would be unlikely to injure him.

Nikon F3, 20mm lens, Fujichrome Professional 100

Ron Kauk's hand on a small hold, Astroman, Yosemite Valley, California; 1985

To get this shot, I used a macro lens and asked Ron to move his face upward into the field of view while I stayed focused on his fingers. I wanted to emphasize the way his fingers clung to almost nothing with a dusting of gymnast's chalk to aid the friction. By having the hand close to the lens, it takes on a much greater apparent size and visual power in relation to the face. The photograph began with a concept I saw in my mind's eye, not with seeing this image before my eyes. In the sense that I asked Ron to pose and move his face into just the right position, it is a controlled photograph rather than a pure documentary one, but this type of image is becoming an ever-greater component of photojournalism.

Nikon F3, 55mm lens, Fujichrome Professional 100

Ron Kauk and Werner Braun after climbing Astroman, Yosemite Valley, California; 1985

When we descended at two in the afternoon after climbing Astroman, Ron and Werner switched into jeans and running shoes in the parking lot. Seeing most of Werner's worldly possessions in the open trunk, I asked if I could take a photograph of Ron sitting there beside it. After I shot a frame or two, Werner decided to walk into the picture playing his guitar, and I caught the candid moment. The image reflects the low-budget carefree lifestyle of resident Yosemite climbers, an unofficially endangered species monitored by the National Park Service with the direct opposite agenda of habitat protection afforded birds and mammals on the list.

Nikon F3, 20mm lens, Fujichrome Professional 100

Figures on a Landscape, Joshua Tree National Monument, California; 1985

The name of this climb is literally Figures on a Landscape because of the way climbers appear at the top of this first pitch. The climb traverses right in the last 30 feet, thus setting up a wonderful visual dynamic in the positions of the two climbers on the route. I was going to climb the route next, but I kept my camera on a tripod until the last moment to capture my friends in this classic position. Yes, I did orchestrate them wearing similar colors to help create the effect I wanted.

Nikon F3, 85mm lens, Fujichrome Professional 50

Clearing storm over El Capitan, Yosemite Valley, California; 1973

At the end of a stormy period in Yosemite, clouds still filled the valley when I went out before dawn to search for coyotes and deer to photograph with a telephoto lens. I had Ektachrome 200 in my camera for the low light and telephotos of wildlife, so that's what I shot for the first few frames when this magical light appeared on El Capitan as the clouds began to lift. Realizing that the moment was very unusual and fleeting, I rewound the fast film out of my camera and put in Kodachrome II (ISO 25). The difference between the same scene on the two films is a classic demonstration of why slow, fine-grained films are best for landscapes. The Ektachrome blocked up the shadows, showing almost no snow on the trees and adding a green cast on the cliff and clouds. The golden mist clinging to the cliff at dawn modeled the contours of El Capitan in a way that I never saw before or since.

Nikon FTN, 24mm lens, Kodachrome II (ISO 25)

Last light on Horsetail Fall, Yosemite, California; 1973

Although this looks like the old Yosemite firefall, the red beam is actually water lit by sunset against the shadowed cliff. For about two days each year, the sun is properly aligned on the horizon to cast the rock wall of the east face of El Capitan in shadow while the out-thrust jet of water catches vivid alpenglow. When there are clouds in the west, not enough snow to feed the waterfall, or too cold temperatures to allow melt, the display doesn't happen. The evening after I first saw it, I was riding around the valley with a high-level ranger. He had never seen the display, and I broke the speed limit racing the light to the base, where I jumped a signed fence with my 300mm lens to get a clear view. Instead of writing one of the longer citations of his career, the ranger looked at the fantastic light and asked, "Is there anything else you need over there?"

"My tripod. It's on the back seat."

He passed it over, and I gave him one of the first prints of a rare natural event that I discovered by accident.

Nikon FTN, 300mm lens, Kodachrome II (ISO 25)

Oak trees in dawn mist, Yosemite Valley, California; 1973

After a storm, the fall air in Yosemite Valley was exceptionally crisp and clear. The meadows were so moist that ground fog appeared as soon as the sun struck the scene. Wandering around the meadow, I was struck by the symmetry of these three trees set against the inclined black ridge in the distance with a wedge of blue sky. I placed the distant tree between the two on the right to add a visual counterpoint that would balance the composition. A polarizer held at nearly a right angle to the sunlight (where it has its maximum effect) helped richen the colors.

Nikon FTN, 50mm lens, Kodachrome II (ISO 25)

Skiers at dawn on the Bighorn Plateau, John Muir Trail, California; 1988

I grew up hearing my mother's tales of hiking the route of the John Muir Trail over the course of three summers in the 1920s before it was completed. Wanting to do it in a different way, I planned a winter ski tour of the route as part of *National Geographic* coverage that also included a spread of old photographs taken by my aunt of my mother's journey. This photo was taken when we were several days into the trip as the full moon set

in the morning sky. I lay down on the snow with a telephoto to silhouette my partners fully against the peaks as they skied ahead.

Nikon F3, 75–150 zoom lens, Fujichrome Professional 50

Moonrise at sunset from Cathedral Peak, Yosemite, California; 1987

I carefully planned this photo for my book, *The Yosemite,* which celebrates the centennial of the park. Quotes by John Muir for each image are used to show how well the essential values he found have been preserved. Because he had made the first ascent of Cathedral Peak in 1869 by a difficult solo climb, I climbed the peak and stayed on top on the evening of a full moon, hoping to catch it rising over Mount Lyell at sunset. I almost gave up and descended when the sky remained overcast throughout the sunset hour, but at the very last moment the sun came out under the clouds in the west. The eastern sky turned vivid pink above the blue earth shadow as the orange glow from the western clouds bathed all the shadowed granite and snow below the peak. I descended into the darkness, fulfilled.

Nikon FM2, 75–150 zoom lens, Fujichrome Professional 50

Moonset at sunrise, Wheeler Crest, Eastern Sierra, California; 1972

This extreme telephoto image was made on New Year's morning, 1972, the clearest day I have ever seen in the Eastern Sierra. After a long storm washed the air, the temperature dropped to −22 degrees Fahrenheit in the community nearest the ridge in this photograph. I had slept beside my car in an open clearing to be in a good position to catch the moon, and as it set I was standing, still in my sleeping bag, beside my tripod. I purposely waited for the full moon to drop just below the horizon, because people had begun to doubt the veracity of photographs. Manipulating full moons into night scenes by double exposure or duplication was already rampant in the undisciplined world of travel photography. Because the moon has the same exposure value as daylight, it can only be photographed with proper detail against a sunlit landscape, as in this fortuitous situation.

Nikon FTN, 500mm lens, Kodachrome II (ISO 25)

Sunrise over Monument Valley, Arizona; 1986

When I awoke well before dawn several miles away from Monument Valley at Gouldings Trading Post, I had a choice of returning to an overlook at the closed gate of the Navajo Tribal Park or trying something new until the gate opened after sunrise. I thought about how I, as well as countless other photographers, had shot almost every possible close view of the main rock formations from the overlook. Only the most unusual light would add a new dimension. The striated cloud patterns in the predawn sky didn't bode well for direct light on the rocks, so I scrambled up the hill behind Gouldings to an open viewpoint where I walked back and forth to compose the most pleasing silhouette. The spires are actually spaced at quite different distances, rather than being in the two-dimensional row that appears in the photograph because of the uniform lighting combined with the compression of a telephoto lens.

Nikon F3, 180mm lens, Fujichrome Professional 50

Oak Creek near Red Rock Crossing, Sedona, Arizona; 1987

When I arrived at Oak Creek on a stormy afternoon, I imagined creating a photograph with a strong foregound that would lead the viewer's eye through the picture. Easier said than done. After searching out opportunities with too much white, which would stop the eye, or too strong horizontal lines in the water, which would lead the eye sideways, I finally stepped out on some rocks and set up my tripod directly in the water. I created a visual sense of flow to match my subject by using a very wide-angle lens turned down toward the water with a graduated neutral-density filter to hold back the exposure on the sunlit sandstone towers.

Nikon F3, 20mm lens, Fujichrome Professional 50

Mule deer at sunset, Thunder Rock Cove, Oregon; 1984

With my camera and 500mm extreme telephoto lens on my tripod, I descended a steep slope to catch an image of the setting sun over the ocean on a clear evening. The thought of making a wildlife photograph didn't occur to me until I heard a noise, spotted this deer in the grass, and quickly turned my camera 180 degrees to focus on the animal in the last light, just as it lifted its head with a catch light reflected in its eye. Over the years I've found that many of my favorite wildlife photographs do not result from portraits of habituated or captive animals staring into my lens but from discovered moments when an image captures a truly wild creature at one with its natural environment.

Nikon F3, 500mm lens, Kodachrome 64

Storm clouds over Peyto Lake, Banff Park, Canadian Rockies; 1982

On a cloudy afternoon I stopped at the Peyto Lake overlook and walked down to the classic viewpoint. The lake has become something of an icon of the Canadian Rockies, almost always depicted in bright sunlight when the turquoise hue is most intense. I had such photographs in my files from many former visits, but I decided to take a few shots anyway with experimental graduated neutral-density filters I was trying out. Thus the bright clouds were held back to approximately the same exposure value as the shadowed lake. *American Photo* magazine later chose this image for its cover, and I learned that with the proper tools, distant landscapes can be dynamically rendered in what many landscape photographers would call poor light.

Nikon F3, 35mm lens, Kodachrome 25

Elk in hot springs mist, Yellowstone National Park, Montana; 1978

While driving through Yellowstone before dawn to catch sunrise light on hot springs, I spotted these elk in the forest and stopped to watch them. In the murky light they blended in with their surroundings to such a degree that I was sure they wouldn't come out in a photograph. Then they stepped into the mist and stood there briefly in bold relief against the whiteness. I braced my telephoto lens on my car's window sill and got off a couple of frames before the elk merged back into the forest again. What sets this image apart from some of my earliest attempts to capture animals in similar ephemeral situations was my conscious effort not to bull's-eye the elk in the middle of the image. Centered pictures of wild creatures call strong subconscious attention to a human-imparted sense of order that destroys the very wildness the image is meant to communicate. Compositions that emphasize nature's randomness, with animals in unexpected parts of the frame, are always more successful, except in rare situations where a strong natural design in the actual scene suggests tuning into it.

Nikon FTN, 400mm lens, Kodachrome 64

Valley of the Ten Peaks, Banff Park, Canadian Rockies; 1973

In several trips back to this same location, I have been unable to achieve anything close to this image. The wildflowers were at the peak of their bloom, with colors enhanced by the moisture of an afternoon thunderstorm that had just passed. The veil of rain between the flowers and the mountains holds back the exposure value to focus attention on the flowers rather than the white sky or snow. The only problem was that the breeze at the end of the storm was rustling the flowers so that the one nearest the camera is blurred. For years I didn't include this shot in my best work because it was technically imperfect, even though my camera had been firmly on a tripod and properly focused with plenty of depth of field. When this image became the Sierra Club's best-selling poster in the early 1980s, it underscored the fact that people judge nature photographs far more by emotional response than by absolute sharpness.

Nikkormat FTN, 35mm lens, Kodachrome II (ISO 25)

Lynx in alpine flowers, Teklanika River, Alaska Range, Alaska; 1974

This image was the first one in my career that made me aware of how many people doubt the veracity of any truly unusual photograph they see. With modern digital manipulation, unscrupulous nature photographers have indeed published radically altered imagery without proper disclosure, but even back in 1974 people told me with certainty that this lynx must be either stuffed, tame, captive, or sick. To the contrary, it was one of the brightest and most alert wild creatures I have ever observed. The lynx actually approached within 30 feet of me in broad daylight before standing tall at the moment I made this shot, only to pounce into a bush and come flying out the back side with a snowshoe rabbit in its mouth. With hindsight and four frames clicked off, I realized that the rabbit's attention had been focused on me, while the lynx had used me as a decoy to complete its stalk.

Nikon FTN, 200mm lens, Kodachrome 64

Skier on the Kahiltna Glacier, Denali National Park, Alaska; 1978

I included the sun in a vast panorama with the silhouette of a skier in order to convey the drama of being all alone on the Kahiltna Glacier at the end of winter. Knowing that my widest 20mm lens would create starlike rays

around the sun at its smallest aperture ($f22$), and add a few polygonal flares caused by internal reflections, I composed the image to point these flares I could barely detect toward the skier in a long diagonal. My exposure was purposely a full stop dark for the sky in order to have the best definition in the sun and snow.

Nikon FM, 20mm lens, Kodachrome 25

View from 16,000 feet, Mount McKinley, Alaska; 1979

I made this photograph on a climb of Mount McKinley a year after circling the peak on skis and doing the first one-day ascent. I had carried only a tiny Minox above 14,000 feet on the one-day climb, but this time I had a Nikon with several lenses and far more time to spare. When a fellow climber walked out of camp to look over the top of a section called The Headwall to see if other climbers were on their way up, I followed him with my camera and caught his moment of contemplation in this hand-held shot. Although I also made images of people at this camp in splendid twilight colors, those failed to convey the broad sense of place that comes across in this more open lighting. At about ten o'clock on a June night with twenty-four-hour daylight on the upper mountain, the low-angled light was just beginning to cast long shadows across the cloud layers below, which would soon destroy this expansive appearance.

Nikon FM, 85mm lens, Kodachrome 25

Massive avalanche on Mount McKinley, Alaska; 1978

We were two weeks into our ski orbit of the mountain when this avalanche dropped 4,000 feet from overhanging ice cliffs onto the Ruth Glacier. I quickly put my telephoto lens on my camera and took this photograph at the moment the wall of ice switched directions after hitting bottom and began advancing across the glacier toward us. I honestly didn't know if it would reach us, but I doubted we could ski away fast enough to make any difference. I had time to zip my camera away in my fanny pack, zip my parka up tight, turn my back to the oncoming cloud, and cover my mouth with my hands just before a dust cloud moving at least 100 miles per hour engulfed us with powder snow. The main force of the avalanche stopped about half a mile out onto the glacier from this photograph, perhaps a full mile from where we spent the next ten minutes calming down and dusting off ourselves and our gear.

Nikon FM, 200mm lens, Kodachrome 25

Jumping a crevasse at the head of Peters Glacier, Alaska; 1978

As our team of four began to descend the steep and icy Peters Glacier from Kahiltna Pass with 90-pound packs and light touring skis without edges, we came to this crevasse with an ice cliff on its upper side. One at a time, we jumped over the lowest point that had a good landing. Thus I was in a perfect position to catch Doug Weins in midair as I held his safety rope from below in one hand and my camera to my eye with the other. The last person lowered our packs on a rope, and we continued to ski.

Nikon FM, 20mm lens, Kodachrome 25

Traversing the Peters Glacier below the NW face of Mount McKinley, Alaska; 1978

On this subzero March day we encountered wild arctic conditions as we tried to ski across the glacier with 90-pound packs in winds gusting to at least 90 knots. Alan Bard was blown over minutes after I took this shot, dislocating his shoulder and almost having to abandon the trip. He skied into a camp pitched early with his arm bound helplessly against his chest. After a night's rest, he considered his options and decided to go on for at least two more weeks to complete the journey.

Nikon FM, 200mm lens, Kodachrome 25

Ned Gillette skiing down Mount McKinley after the first one-day ascent, Alaska; 1978

Ned and I used short mountaineering skis with climbing skins for the first 3,500 feet of our climb, then cached them and finished our round-trip with a superb downhill run through icefalls and snow bowls, passing crevasses at points we had carefully checked out on our ascent. This photograph was hand-held with a short telephoto lens at a place where I asked Ned to stop and ski by me. I purposely composed it with tight croping behind his feet, but with space in front to show where he was headed. I had also cached the Nikon FM that I used to take this photograph with my skis, a decision I now regret because the tiny Minox I took higher failed in the extreme cold near the top.

Nikon FM, 105mm lens, Kodachrome 25

Aerial view of Ruth Gorge, Denali National Park, Alaska; 1986

When I was invited to photograph for *A Day in the Life of America,* I requested Alaska. On the big day I made a predawn flight with my friend Doug Geeting, a bush pilot working out of Talkeetna, Alaska. I was especially interested in capturing the granite walls of the Ruth Gorge beneath the pink and indigo glow of twilight. I had spent months camping, climbing, and skiing in the gorge on four expeditions during the seventies, but all of my aerial photographs had been in boring direct light. With the highest granite walls on the continent, the Ruth Gorge seems like an outsized Yosemite Valley in the Pleistocene, still locked in ice with cliffs much higher than El Capitan rising directly from the glacier for a vertical mile.

Nikon F3, 35mm lens, Kodachrome 64

Barbara Rowell flying her Cessna near Mount McKinley, Alaska; 1986

Two years after she got her pilot's license, my wife, Barbara, asked me to be her passenger on a flying adventure north of the Arctic Circle from our home in California. When we stopped in Talkeetna, Alaska, local bush pilot and old friend Doug Geeting helped set up this scene by having her fly beside the sheer granite faces of the Ruth Gorge while I photographed through the open window of his airplane. I used a short telephoto lens and the fastest shutter speed I could get—1/500th second—to stop the motion.

Nikon F3, 85mm lens, Kodachrome 64

View from inside a crevasse after a fall, Mount Dickey, Alaska; 1974

Before attempting the unclimbed mile-high Southeast Face of Mount Dickey without a tent or food for more than four days, the three of us climbed the much easier backside of the peak to leave a small cache for our descent. We also wanted to find the best route off the peak in case of a storm. As I was leading up a smooth snow slope about as steep as an expert ski run, the ground opened up and I plunged into a hidden crevasse. After 35 feet, the rope, tied to my two companions above, stopped me. When David Roberts cautiously peered into the hole to see how I was doing, I recognized a great photograph and told him to hold the pose until I could shoot a picture with the camera I had in a chest pouch.

Nikkormat FTN, 35mm lens, Kodachrome 64

Cabin in the Don Sheldon Amphitheater, Alaska Range, Alaska; 1978

I first visited this cabin with the legendary bush pilot Don Sheldon, who had built it because it made a great place to bring clients—both mountaineers and flightseers—and because with a federal permit for the cabin he would be able to land his airplane there, even if the proposed southern extension to Denali National Park were to ban ski-plane landings in the region. I took this picture four years later, after Sheldon had died of cancer. I set my camera on a piece of cut firewood I stuck in the snow and exposed for four minutes to get the night sky and glow of the fire in the cabin.

Nikon FM, 24mm lens, Kodachrome 64

Alaskan brown bear mother and cub, McNeil River, Alaska; 1979

Mothers with young cubs are very wary around the McNeil River falls, where the greatest known concentration of grizzlies in the world gathers each summer to fish for salmon. Grizzlies are the world's worst fathers, ready to devour any cub—including their own—that is momentarily unprotected by its mother. This grizzly act benefits the bad dad by bringing the female immediately into estrus and potentially removing another bear's offspring from the gene pool, thus upping its own contribution to future generations. I spotted this mother bear sitting by the falls, patiently waiting for enough of the thirty-one bears I saw at once to satiate themselves and move on so that she and her cub could move in for a meal. I caught the moment her cub put his head on her haunches with my camera and very long lens set up on a tripod at the sidelines, guarded by an armed game warden.

Nikon FTN, 600mm lens, Kodachrome 64

Reflection Pond, Denali National Park, Alaska; 1986

This pond was named for its fabulous reflections of Mount McKinley on clear days. I never would have guessed that my favorite image would turn out to be one of the pond in which the mountain was not visible at all. Just before sunrise on a fall morning, I drove to the pond with hopes of a clear shot of the peak. After waiting past the time of first light on the peak, I left and began looking for wildlife. Half an hour later, one corner of the sky turned clear. Even though a mass of clouds blocked all views of the mountain, I had a hunch that something wonderful might happen back at the pond. Stratus clouds turned pink and were reflected as I set up my tripod a moment before the grasses in the pond were struck by direct sunlight. This also made the wet leaves and berries glisten. With my lens set at *f*22 for maximum depth of field, I only had time to click off two exposures before the light suddenly went flat again.

Nikon F3, 20mm lens, Fujichrome Professional 50

Sunset over the Knik River, Alaska; 1988

Spring in Alaska begins to arrive with the break up of ice on frozen rivers. One of the earliest to go is the lower Knik where it meets the huge tides of Cook Inlet. One evening when an especially good sunset seemed likely, I drove out of Anchorage toward Palmer and walked out on a bridge over the river. I positioned myself above some very large ice flows that tended to reflect the blue of the midsky rather than the orange of the western horizon. With a graduated neutral-density filter to preserve detail in the shadows, I maximized the color saturation of warm versus cool tones in this otherworldly scene.

Nikon F3, 24mm lens, Fujichrome Professional 50

Icebergs in a storm, Portage Glacier, Alaska; 1980

On a blustery fall day after the summer tourists were gone from the Portage Glacier area south of Anchorage, I found a group of icebergs blown to one side of a lake. I had been there many times and had never seen a grouping anything like this. Even though the lighting seemed too flat and bluish for normal landscapes, this cool blue was just what I needed to emphasize the tones of the icebergs. I used a telephoto lens and a low camera angle to home in on the bergs in the mist. The rich blue of the resulting slide exceeded my expectations, and the image turned out to be one of my favorites.

Nikon F3, 24mm lens, Kodachrome 25

Riders beneath giant sand dune, Pamir Range, China; 1980

I came across this dune at 13,000 feet along the ancient Silk Road while traveling with the first American expedition allowed into China's "Wild West" by the Communist government of the People's Republic. In the thirteenth century, Marco Polo had marveled at this same landscape on his way to visit the

Great Khan. Seeing two riders in the distance, I guessed that they might come close to the dune at the edge of a meadow, because that's what I would have done myself. I skipped breakfast with my fellow climbers and waited with my sharpest telephoto lens perched "rock steady" on top of a rock wall—braced with pebbles to aim the camera. Using Kodachrome 25 to muster every bit of film sharpness, I made several exposures at *f*8, the lens' sharpest aperture. The image ran across two pages in *National Geographic* and across 6 feet in the entry hall mural of a traveling exhibit.

Nikon F3, 180mm lens, Kodachrome 25

Shrine on Mount Tateyama, Japan Alps, Japan; 1985

This image became the frontispiece of *A Day in the Life of Japan,* after I had conceived it in my mind before climbing the mountain at night to be there at sunrise. I figured that a sunrise shot had a chance to be the lead photo of a book about a day in a country. I asked around about a mountain that would have something on top that would be clearly Japanese. Friends told me of the ancient Shinto shrine from A.D. 703 atop Mount Tateyama, so I scouted it on the day before the shoot and figured out exactly where I wanted to be at dawn. I brought a friend to pose in profile on top and combined the Shinto arch in silhouette with the diffraction star of the sun as it came around the corner of the peak at the break of dawn.

Nikon F3, 55mm lens, Fujichrome Professional 50

Spring breakup on Lake Baikal, Siberia; 1987

When I arrived at this fabled lake in early May with only one day to scout and one to shoot, conditions were awful. High winds and blowing snow hampered photography, while pack ice floating on the lake made travel by boat hazardous. Except for one ride across an open bay, I was confined to the shore, where mud and vegetation made for distracting foregrounds. During a brief clearing, I found a place where I could walk out on an ice flow and set up my tripod at the edge. Winds were rippling the surface, but a polarizer removed enough reflections to give the water a clear, brush-stroked look, as if it were a painted tableau. A graduated neutral-density filter handheld over the polarizer kept the sky dark as I opened up my exposure to show the rocks at the bottom of the lake.

Nikon F3, 35mm lens, Fujichrome Professional 50

Austrian Camp, Annapurna Himal, Nepal; 1987

As the Annapurna Range began to turn pink in the setting sun, I positioned myself at the edge of the meadow where we were camped. Using a graduated neutral-density filter to open up the foreground exposure, I shot a wide-angle landscape of a scene that has become something of an icon of trekking in Nepal. It ran in my *National Geographic* story on the Annapurna Conservation Area Project, as well as on a popular postcard in Kathmandu.

Nikon F3, 35mm lens, Fujichrome Professional 50

Winter on the Great Wall of China, China; 1983

Most photographs of the Great Wall show it surrounded by verdant spring vegetation. I also saw it that way on my first visit in 1980. When I returned in early March 1983 to climb Mount Everest through Tibet, the wall was snowbound in a barren scene without a leaf on a bush or tree. I needed a visual device to break the flat appearance of the scene and found it in lines of snow running on ledges on the outside of the wall. At a chosen site I leaned over with my camera and wide-angle lens on a tripod. The wall had also lost all perspective of size, so I waited for a group of people to appear at midrange to give it scale.

Nikon F3, 20mm lens, Kodachrome 25

Sand dunes in the Skardu Valley, Pakistan; 1984

The sand dunes of Skardu are quite unexpected beneath the great snow peaks of the Karakoram Himalaya. After venturing onto them, I felt as if I were among the dunes of the San Juan Range in Colorado. Nothing in the scene was a cue to the exotic location until I spotted a Balti family and began to follow them with my camera on a tripod. Here they are starting to walk across open sand into a purple veil of haze that colors the more distant peaks. I sought out such a meeting place of colors and human figures to give the image as much visual power as possible.

Nikon F3, 85mm lens, Kodachrome 25

Kayaking the narrows of the Braldu Gorge, Pakistan; 1984

Treacherous waters flowing out of the Baltoro Glacier below K2 have carved this wild slot canyon out of hard granitic gneiss. A world-class kayaker died minutes after putting his boat in the water on the first attempt to run the Braldu River. I got this shot on the later, first successful running of the river by positioning myself with a tripod on the brink of the chasm as the boats of my expedition came through. Although this "slot of no return" was tricky, it was one of the easier and more predictable sections of the river.

Nikon F3, 35mm lens, Kodachrome 64

Moonlight at Concordia, Karakoram Himalaya, Pakistan; 1975

Concordia is known as one of the great power spots of the mountains of the world. Six major glaciers come together beneath six of the seventeen highest peaks in the world. After most of the other members of the 1975 American K2 Expedition had gone to bed, I ventured out with my camera on a tripod in temperatures around 10 degrees Fahrenheit. My tent was in the shadow of the moonlight, which had just struck the porters' camp below, where twenty-five Baltis were crammed into each four-man umbrella tent with fires alongside to stay warm. They typically remove their home-spun woolen clothing and lay it over the top of a pile of intertwined humanity to sleep in the cold. With only a few minutes to go before the moonlight would reach me and add too much visual emphasis on the foreground, I started bracketing long exposures up to three minutes with a very fast 35mm ƒ1.4 lens. I composed the scene to have convergence of the lines of the glacier arcing around the corner, the range of peaks at left disappearing into the distance, and stars streaking across the sky in the same direction from the earth's movement. With a more modern Nikon F3, I could have simply put the camera on auto exposure, plugged in a slight compensation for the film reciprocity at slow speeds, and walked away. With a manual exposure system, I had to guess. My longest exposure was still a bit on the dark side.

Nikon FTN, 35mm lens, Kodachrome 25

Skiing the upper Siachen Glacier at nearly 20,000 feet, Karakoram Himalaya, Pakistan; 1980

On a moderate winter day with the temperature around 0 degrees Fahrenheit, my four-man expedition was headed toward Conway Saddle, soon to become, at 20,500 feet, the highest year-round human settlement in history when the Siachen Glacier War broke out in 1984. For the duration of our journey on the ice, however, we saw no one else. Having the inner Karakoram entirely to ourselves was a rare experience that I tried my best to record on film. Because of crevasse danger on the glacier, we stayed roped. Most of my images, like this one, hint at my own presence by the rope running out of the frame toward the camera. For this shot, I handheld my camera and asked my companions to ski on as if I had not stopped.

Nikon FM, 35mm lens, Kodachrome 64

The Biafo Glacier from the air, Karakoram Himalaya, Pakistan; 1975

While on the 1975 American K2 Expedition, we made a reconnaissance flight in a military C130 Hercules to the mountain. I made this image of the Ogre and Latok peaks rising above the broad Biafo Glacier from one of the several window positions in the cockpit. Minutes later, as we neared K2 itself, expedition leader Jim Whittaker ordered me away from the window while others, including his wife, continued to shoot. Having an assignment to cover the climb and the mountain for *National Geographic,* I was mortified, but after the attempt on K2 failed, I began looking at the photographs I had made of the great glaciers with a new eye toward putting together a ski mountaineering expedition to traverse the Karakoram Range. This particular scene was clearly in my mind as we descended the most rugged part of the Baltoro Glacier. Knowing that the snow cover had been this good at the start of May gave me confidence that we would have relative smooth sailing on the latter part of our journey in April.

Nikon FM, 35mm lens, Kodachrome 64

Camp on the Siachen Glacier, Karakoram Himalaya, Pakistan; 1980

When I got up shortly after dawn to take this photograph on an absolutely clear and still winter morning, the temperature was –27 degrees Fahrenheit. The previous evening had been snowing and blowing. We had skied up the glacier a ways, looking for a more protected camp, but didn't find one and returned to this flat spot slightly more out of the wind. No winter expedition had ever been in these high peaks before, and no summer expedition had been allowed into the politically sensitive border area for a number of years. Thus the Indian army was able to move onto the glacier unseen in 1984 and occupy a large area formerly claimed on maps by Pakistan. I found myself in the middle of the political dispute because we had procured our 1980 permission through Pakistan only and had had no reason to believe that we should approach the Indian government at the time. The glacier was closed for a number of years, until the Indian government began inviting expeditions to come to bolster their own land claim.

Nikon FM, 24mm lens, Kodachrome 64

Kim Schmitz on the Karakoram Winter Ski Traverse, Pakistan; 1980

Kim was my favorite climbing partner on six Himalayan expeditions we shared together during the seventies and eighties. As we boiled water for tea in our tent on a –27 degrees Fahrenheit morning (the same one as in the above photograph), I took a handheld portrait of his slightly frosted face with a short telephoto lens. Sunlight through the yellow tent gives the image its warm glow.

Nikon FM, 105mm lens, Kodachrome 64

Skiing the Siachen Glacier near Sia La, Karakoram Himalaya, Pakistan; 1980

While Kim Schmitz and I were skiing roped together in a snow storm on the Siachen Glacier, I wanted to get a photo of our other roped team—Dan Asay and Ned Gillette—as tiny figures in the mist below the icefalls of unnamed peaks. We verged onto a separate route a hundred yards from them, and I used a short telephoto lens to compress the perspective of the scene. My camera was carried in a chest pouch always at the ready with three extra lenses stored in a hip sack.

Nikon FM, 105mm lens, Kodachrome 64

Kim Schmitz, Ned Gillette, and Galen Rowell at the end of the Karakoram Winter Ski Traverse, Pakistan; 1980

By the end of our trip we had each lost more than 25 pounds off our already lean frames. We looked like prisoners of war, and our senses were similarly dulled by the mental and physical trauma of moving day after day through the heart of the most continuous high-altitude region on earth under our own power without native porters. The journey had taken us from near the Indian border across northern Pakistan to Hunza—three-fourths of the way to Afghanistan. When we finally took off our skis for the last time as we approached the village of Hispar, I set up a camera with a self-timer to make this photograph.

Nikon FM, 105mm lens, Kodachrome 64

Self-portrait in helicopter, Siachen Glacier War, Karakoram Himalaya, Pakistan; 1984

As my team skied alone across the Siachen Glacier in 1984, I would never have imagined in my wildest dreams that my next sight would be of a war zone from a Pakistan army helicopter. Pakistani soldiers in North Face down suits occupied Conway Saddle at 20,500 feet, the highest year-round camp in history, equipped with Chinese antiaircraft machine guns and U.S. Stinger missiles bought on the black market from European arms dealers. Indian soldiers in Swiss-made down suits occupied a camp just across a big icefall on the Siachen Glacier with Soviet Sam-7 missiles. I viewed the whole scene from a French-made helicopter hovering in a potential line of fire at 21,000 feet. With my camera held in my hand at arm's length, I shot this self-portrait for the record.

Nikon F3, 20mm lens, Fujichrome Professional 50

Pakistani soldiers stationed on the upper Baltoro Glacier, Siachen Glacier War, Karakoram Himalaya, Pakistan; 1984

I had only minutes to jump out of a helicopter at extreme altitudes and photograph soldiers while the aircraft shuttled men and supplies back and forth to the Conway Saddle at 20,500 feet, where 20 percent of the soldiers died of high-altitude pulmonary or cerebral edema during the first two years. I helped load a body into the helicopter at the same site where these men were watching for Indian planes or troops with 50-caliber antiaircraft machine guns. One soldier told me, "We are fighting two enemies: India and Allah. Allah is winning." In 1995 as I am writing these notes, neither Allah nor India has won yet and the war continues with 10,000 men stationed in the mountains.

Nikon F3, 24mm lens, Fujichrome Professional 50

Crescent moon and unnamed peak, Savoia Glacier, Karakoram Himalaya, Pakistan; 1975

The apparent simplicity of this image belies the major technical and aesthetic complications of creating it. When I saw a crescent moon beside the corniced ridge of a peak, I took it as a challenge to see if I could make a fine image. Even though the moon was at least eight stops brighter than the peak an hour after sunset, I figured that the scene had potential for an extreme telephoto lens. A burned-out thin crescent is still pleasing to the eye. We look for detail within the moon to validate our impression of a full moon, but we look only at the outline of a crescent moon. The problem was that the thirty-second exposure I needed for the mountain with my ƒ8 mirror-reflex 500mm lens and ISO 64 film would blur the moon because of movement. I calculated that I needed eight seconds or less not to blur the outline, so I bracketed a number of exposures around four and eight seconds, chose a slide with sharp detail but at least two stops of underexposure, and brightened it back to where I wanted on duplicating film. I called it my secret Kodachrome 400.

Nikon FTN, 500mm lens, Kodachrome 64

Mount Everest by moonlight, Tibet; 1981

In 1981 I was leader of the first American trekking group permitted by the People's Republic of China to go to the Mount Everest Base Camp on the Tibetan side. After we camped at 16,500 feet near Rongbuk Monastery for a night, I climbed to the North Col at 23,000 feet in two days with one very fit member of my group. After I returned, we had a very clear, moonlit night, so I set up my camera on a tripod to make this portrait of the peak just after sunset when the light was still bright, but bluish and very even.

Nikon FM, 105mm lens, Kodachrome 64

Climber on the West Ridge of Mount Everest, Tibet; 1983

A climber ascends the West Ridge from the Tibetan side within one of the huge snow banners caused by extreme winds that are so often seen on the mountain from a distance on "clear" days. No snow is actually falling, but the entire surface of the rippled ice is covered by a ground blizzard that chills hands and feet at the same time that it hides natural features. Here a fixed rope between camps ensures not getting lost or falling on a route that had not been previously attempted from this side of the mountain. I shot this from beside our Camp Two with a long telephoto lens on a tripod. I opened up my exposure by 0.7 stop—just enough to whiten the snow without losing the strength of the figure as a silhouette in the harsh lighting contrasts of high altitudes.

Nikon F3, 600mm lens, Kodachrome 64

Buried tent on the West Ridge of Mount Everest, Tibet; 1983

After not using this camp for just two days during a wind storm, we returned to find our tents completely buried in deep snow. We had previously dug out a large platform, but the winds deposited enough snow to fill in the slope close to its old contour. While we are getting close to excavating the first tent, the second one behind it remains totally buried with 5 feet of snow over the top. Shoveling at high altitude is a very slow process due to the lack of oxygen. We traded off frequently, which gave me time to take out my camera and record the action.

Nikon F3, 35mm lens, Kodachrome 64

American Everest West Expedition below the West Ridge of Mount Everest, Tibet; 1983

After two months on Mount Everest, our team admitted failure due to two weeks of unusually early snow storms that dumped several feet of snow on the peak that did not go away. Comparing the white snow peak depicted in this photograph with the rock peak on pages 88 and 89 that greeted our arrival in March shows the graphic contrast of the change. Bare rock and ice that we had easily scrambled up with crampons on our boots became 3 feet of mashed potatoes, ready to avalanche anew after each wind storm. We had been attempting the West Ridge through Tibet for the first time without native porters or supplementary oxygen. I conceived of this photograph of our team stripped down to underwear in the near-zero temperatures to display the 20 to 30 pounds each of us had lost and make us look as skinny as a starving group of natives. But I misjudged how powerfully built and fit our group remained, even after our ordeal.

Nikon F3, 105mm lens, Kodachrome 64

Base Camp by moonlight beneath the West Ridge of Mount Everest, Tibet; 1983

On a clear evening after we arrived at our 17,000-foot base camp, I set up my camera for a fifteen-minute exposure. While the shutter was open, I walked through the scene, knowing that my figure would not be recorded in the dim light. I opened each tent door and asked permission to set off my flash. The momentary burst of light records on film very much the same way that a dimmer flashlight or lantern would record during such a long exposure, creating tents glowing in the night. I used a Nikon F3 set in automatic exposure mode with a plus 1.5 exposure compensation for film reciprocity at such very slow shutter speeds.

Nikon F3, 85mm lens, Kodachrome 64

Barbara Rowell camped on the east side of Mount Everest, Tibet; 1988

An extremely wide 16mm lens captures my wife, Barbara, reading in her well-organized tent while local Tibetans peer into the doorway. We spent lots of time interacting with the local people, but they never tired of perching themselves on our doorstep for hours at a time to catch a glimpse of our strange and exotic way of life. The East Face of Everest had only been approached a few times before, mainly by another pass to the west. Our interpreter told us that several of these villagers had never seen a foreigner's camp up close before.

Nikon F3, 16mm lens, Fujichrome Professional 100

Entering the Kama Valley on the east side of Mount Everest, Tibet; 1988

In 1988, *National Geographic* sent me to cover the Tibetan side of Mount Everest to document a proposed joint Everest national park with the Nepalese that never happened. On the east side of the peak beyond the village of Kharta, a lone German came through our camp, hiking at quite a fast pace. I invited him to take tea in my camp with an entourage of Chinese forestry officials who were not about to cross the snowy pass. He looked distinctly uncomfortable. I joined him on part of his trek after he told me about his plans. He was doing a complete circling of the peak with no permissions, which would not have been forthcoming from the Chinese on the Tibetan side. A touted American orbit of the peak some years before had been done in two stages with large uncrossed gaps near both borders. For three days we hiked through deep rhododendron forests in bloom, punctuated by organized logging camps that the Chinese government would not acknowledge. I returned alone to my entourage, while my friend completed his journey.

Nikon F3, 24mm lens, Fujichrome Professional 100

Tibetan women carrying fresh timber on the east side of Mount Everest, Tibet; 1988

When *National Geographic* sent me to Tibet to document the proposed national park described above, I found villagers engaged in a Chinese-controlled logging operation that exported finished lumber to the rest of woodless Tibet to build more Chinese infrastructure. These women were carrying beams that weighed more than 100 pounds over a 16,300-foot pass from the lush Kama Valley that gets more than 200 inches of rain per year. Thus instead of documenting the great beauty of a pristine region, I came back with many images that showed the systematic destruction of some of Tibet's last virgin forests. Bill Thompson, the photographer on the Nepal side, brought back similar coverage. When we convinced the editors that the park was not going to happen any time soon, our joint coverage ran in November 1988 under the title "Heavy Hands on the Land." I later used this photograph in a cover story for *Greenpeace* that brought about public awareness for the first time of broad-based Tibetan environmental abuses that are on a scale with the cultural destruction of this sacred nation.

Nikon F3, 20mm lens, Fujichrome Professional 100

Sunset on Machapuchare, Annapurna Region, Nepal; 1987

Moments after I shot the camp scene on pages 66–67, I dropped over the bluff on the right edge of the meadow to a spot where I had stomped out a tripod platform an hour before. I had planned to shoot the tented meadow first while light was more fully on the peaks to illuminate a broad scenic. Then I would isolate the peak of Machapuchare in the last light with a single tree profiled against the meeting place of alpenglow and deep blue shadows. I used a graduated neutral-density filter to open up detail in the foreground while holding saturation on the mountain itself.

Nikon F3, 85mm lens, Fujichrome Professional 50

Sunrise in Khumjung, Khumbu Region, Nepal; 1982

While camped on the edge of this Sherpa village on the classic Mount Everest trek, I wandered out before dawn with my camera. I found a spot where I could silhouette a Buddhist chorten and put the rising sun in a gap on

the summit ridge of a high peak to cause rays to diffract in a star pattern. As the sun rose, I kept moving my tripod position closer to keep the sun in the gap. After I had shot a number of variations, two women on their way to the fields walked into my frame and I caught them just as they were fully profiled against the mountain.

Nikon F3, 55mm lens, Kodachrome 64

Sunset on Cholatse, Khumbu Region, Nepal; 1978

I made this photograph in 1978 when I trekked up the Gokyo Valley to a vantage point for sunset photographs of Mount Everest. From our camp near Gokyo Lake, Cholatse was a far more impressive mountain, although it was more than 8,000 feet lower. Four years later I joined a small expedition that made the first ascent of the peak via the southwest ridge at the far right of this photograph. We made three bivouacs on the upper mountain, which was composed of much harder ice than we had expected. The weather was never clear, and even though I spent two weeks in the vicinity of the mountain to climb it, I never got as good a photo of it as on my first trip four years earlier.

Nikon FM, 105mm lens, Kodachrome 64

Swayambu Temple, Kathmandu, Nepal; 1987

Every time I visit Nepal I do morning runs up to Swayambu Temple at dawn. On this particular morning the rest of the town was in fog, but as I came up the hill to the temple, the sun was breaking through. I stood up on a railing so as not to have parallax distortion that would make the temple seem to be falling over. I braced the camera on a post and waited for what seemed like the best moment. Street merchants and groups of Hindu people walking together lacked the simplicity and visual power of this woman and a single monk circumambulating the holy shrine in separate thought worlds.

Nikon F3, 20mm lens, Ektachrome 100 Plus Professional

Robert Redford and Barbara Rowell at the Swayambu Temple, Nepal; 1982

In the fall of 1982, Barbara and I traveled through Nepal for a month with Robert Redford to show him the country. Because of his involvement with American Indians, particularly the

Hopi, he was especially interested in Himalayan native people. One morning before dawn the three of us went to Swayambu Temple to see the Buddhist and Hindu worshippers use the ancient shrine concurrently. Two women were sitting below a giant bronze dorje, which is a male fertility symbol. They ignored us as intruders into their usual morning solitude—just another bunch of boring tourists. I caught the moment with a telephoto lens from the side, chuckling to myself about how differently American woman respond to Redford's presence.

Nikon F3, 105mm lens, Kodachrome 64

Balti in a dust storm, Karakoram Himalaya, Pakistan; 1975

I shot this image out of the back of a moving jeep at 1/1,000 second with my lens wide open. I saw the scene coming as we were about to pass a barefoot Balti native wearing a homespun robe of goats' wool in the blowing sand. At the last moment he turned his head away to avoid the increased wake of sand from our vehicle. Catching him midstride captured the feeling of a race of native people very much in balance with their land, despite the surrounding political turmoil. Captivating shots like this where the subject's and the camera's motion in opposite directions are frozen into a moment worthy of contemplation make me risk a very low success ratio to shoot from moving cars, boats, planes, horses, and the like.

Nikkormat FTN, 105mm lens, Kodachrome 64

Moslem women, Shigar, Baltistan, Pakistan; 1984

As my expedition headed off in jeeps across the Skardu Valley to begin the long trek up the gorge of the Braldu River that leads to K2, we stopped at the village of Shigar to take pictures of a mosque. It was filled with praying Balti men—only men. In the distance, we could see the women of the village going about their daily tasks, but closer to us, they had ceased working. One of these two women had covered herself with a veil, while the other sat on the stairs, looking away. I put my camera on a tripod and composed a scene of visual tension with emptiness near the middle and the two women pushed out into opposite corners of the frame. They seemed to blend into the wall of the building as they sequestered themselves from the eyes of unrelated men in the firm tradition of their faith. To me this was a far more significant photograph than one I might

sneak with a telephoto lens behind a tree of an unveiled woman.

Nikon F3, 200mm lens, Kodachrome 64

Girl in a window, Srinigar, Vale of Kashmir, India; 1977

Srinigar has recently become known to the world as a place of fighting and strife where a foreign tourist is in great danger. The situation my Nun Kun Expedition found in 1977 was far more peaceful. The Vale looked like a long slab of jade set between the mountains. Rice fields and canals lined with poplars surrounded a city called the Venice of Asia because of its floating markets and hundreds of gondola-like shikaras on inland waterways. On a morning walk I was somewhat disappointed to find the inner city squalid and undistinguished, like finding part of Harlem beneath the Tetons in Wyoming. As I walked down an alley, I noticed a young girl staring at me from a second-story window. I thought I would be lucky to get one shot with a long telephoto lens, but after I grabbed a rather poor one from behind a wall, she did not avert her gaze when I came out in the open. The slats on the window were as a veil to her, and I was able to shoot two very sharp, carefully composed images of her before smiling my appreciation and moving on.

Nikon FM, 200mm lens, Kodachrome 64

Punjabi merchant, Rawalpindi, Pakistan; 1975

When the 1975 American K2 Expedition arrived in Pakistan, a period of bad weather prevented us from flying to Skardu in the mountains for eleven days. Almost every morning I walked the teeming markets of Rawalpindi, sensing echoes of Kipling's fabled descriptions of this ancient town. By the second or third day, merchants would greet me with a smile or a "Salaam Sahib." One day, I stopped for several minutes in an area where this dignified merchant kept watching me without comment. When I turned my camera his way, his neighbors talked to him in Urdu, which I couldn't understand. From the tone and the outcome, they were clearly urging him to sit still for his portrait, rather than to turn away, like so many of his peers when tourists point cameras their way. My best photos of people virtually always happen after some sort of extended exchange establishes a relationship and confirms their dignity.

Nikon FTN, 200mm lens, Kodachrome 64

Oyongo village, Braldu Valley, Baltistan, Pakistan; 1984

The inner sanctum of the Karakoram Himalaya was only accessible by trails that zigzagged along sheer canyon walls on the earliest of my nine journeys into these mountains. In the eighties, however, the government began to construct a road 35 miles up the gorge to the highest village of Askole. Frequent landslides stopped progress, and when I made this photograph in 1984 the road passed through Oyongo, but hadn't been used yet. Thus the village was still locked in the Middle Ages, as I had first seen it, but major change was on the verge of happening. Merchants from the lowlands would come to establish stores throughout Baltistan in years to come. Television and videocassette recorders would immediately follow electrification. I feel lucky to have experienced this land and its people as I first saw them. Oyongo owes its existence among the barren cliffs to a single canal from a glacier-fed stream that waters a myriad of terraces lined with apricot, mulberry, and poplar trees. The road can be seen at the base of the hillside, awaiting completion.

Nikon F3, 55mm lens, Kodachrome 64

Shangrila resort, Skardu Valley, Baltistan, Pakistan; 1986

Just after the end of the 1947-48 Pakistan-India War, an Orient Airlines DC-3 crash-landed in the sands of the level Skardu Valley. The passengers escaped, and a war hero named Brigadier Aslam Khan, who had acquired some land at the end of the valley, negotiated to buy the remains. He paid the equivalent of seventeen dollars in rupees and hired local people to tow the plane onto his land, where he used it as a hunting cabin for several decades. When I did a *National Geographic* story on Baltistan, I spent a week at the Brigadier's new Shangri-la Resort, where the plane had become the honeymoon suite. When the sky was overcast and the lighting soft, I climbed up to get a high, diagonal view of the incongruous plane with a wide-angle lens.

Nikon F3, 20mm lens, Fujichrome Professional 50

Star streaks over Mount Kailas, Western Tibet; 1987

I never would have made this image of the stars over this sacred mountain without holding an image in my mind's eye that guided me. As I thought about how to make a unique portrait of the mountain, I kept in mind that Tibetan Buddhists and Hindus consider it to be the earthly manifestation of mythical Mount Meru, the center of the universe. To show it that way, I imagined an arc of stars streaking across the heavens with the peak pointing skyward. A fifteen-minute exposure on a tripod with a 24mm lens on my camera gave me enough moonlight on the peak combined with enough streaking of the stars, from the earth's rotation.

Nikon F3, 24mm lens, Kodachrome 25

Moonrise over Lake Manasarovar, Western Tibet; 1987

When my small group left Lhasa to travel a thousand miles overland to explore the source of the Brahmaputra River for *National Geographic,* one of my main goals was to reach the region in time to photograph the full moon rising at sunset. A week later, I arrived within the hour. When the moon appeared in the still-red sky on the horizon, I had my camera ready at the edge of this holy lake near the sources of both the Indus and the Brahmaputra rivers. A graduated neutral-density filter helped open up the blue tones of the lake while preserving detail in the moon and sky.

Nikon F3, 200mm lens, Fujichrome Professional 50

End of the pilgrimage route around Mount Kailas, Western Tibet; 1987

As I began the 34-mile pilgrimage trail around sacred Mount Kailas, I spotted unnaturally bright colors on a broad ledge and climbed up to a vast area of apparently discarded personal items. A Tibetan from India in my party who spoke English explained that when pilgrims complete the circle, they leave material belongings from their former life behind to underscore the spiritual change they have undergone. I used a tripod and wide-angle lens to emphasize the vast panorama of items spread across the landscape with the holy mountain rising above it all. The pilgrimage route follows the bottom of the steep-walled canyon beneath the mountain.

Nikon F3, 20mm lens, Fujichrome Professional 50

Lammergeier hovering near Mount Kailas, Western Tibet; 1987

These huge birds have been called the Tibetan counterpart of our condor. With wingspreads of more than 9 feet, they can soar effortlessly for hours at high altitudes. Tibetans consider the lammergeier to be quite smart and dignified, for a vulture. The birds have been observed dropping bare bones onto rocks from a great height to break them apart and get to the marrow. They are an integral part of Tibetan "celestial" burials, in which the deceased are cut into pieces and left atop large rocks where the birds come to take the bodies to the heavens. This lammergeier was near a site where I found parts of the bodies of several Kailas pilgrims left out on the rocks. When it swooped low, I caught its glance with a handheld telephoto lens.

Nikon F3, 180mm lens, Fujichrome Professional 100

Pilgrims prostrating around Mount Kailas, Western Tibet; 1987

A Buddhist pilgrimage is based upon willingly experiencing physical hardship for spiritual reward. Many types of Western adventurers also fit this same description, although we tend to describe ourselves far less in terms of our spiritual gains than by the act we do to get there—trekking, climbing, skiing, or running. Just as climbing the face of a peak requires more physical commitment than walking up a trail on the other side, prostrating a pilgrimage route rather than walking is harder and thus produces a higher degree of spiritual merit. When I stopped to photograph these pilgrims, who would take three weeks to complete the 34-mile holy *kora* around Kailas by their chosen method, I was running the same circular pilgrimmage route in one day with my camera. By the end of my run, which had started as a moonlight fast walk with Tibetans, I had been drawn completely out of my Western shell into a spiritual connection with the land.

Nikon FM2, 24mm lens, Fujichrome Professional 100

Mother and child cresting the Dolma La at 18,600 feet, Mount Kailas, Western Tibet; 1987

When I saw this young girl in a sheepskin *chuba* walking through the snow on the crest of a Tibetan pass, my heart went out to her. She was so intent on what she was doing that she never looked up when I walked over and photographed her reaching the top. I later selected the image as a candidate for my book with the Dalai Lama, *My Tibet.* When I projected it for His Holiness on a screen at his home, he smiled broadly and said these words that we quoted under the image in the book: "This child of Western Tibet may not have much understanding of what a pilgrimage is about, but, you see, we Buddhists believe that merit is accumulated when you take part in something religious even though it may be without full understanding. Internally, the proper attitude is being shaped."

Nikon FM2, 75–150mm lens, Fujichrome Professional 50

Pilgrim on the way to Mount Kailas, Western Tibet; 1987

As Tsewang Tsambu and I traveled together toward Mount Kailas, he became quite comfortable with my photography. Through an interpreter, I asked him to pretend I didn't exist, even when he looked my way, if I was taking a photograph. This came naturally to a person who spends his life practicing the belief that all external phenomena are empty of inherent existence. Here he was heating a pot of water over a yak-dung fire to brew tea just after getting up on a 10-degree morning at 15,000 feet.

Nikon F3, 24mm lens, Fujichrome Professional 50

Nomad family of Pekhu Tso, Western Tibet; 1988

A year after traveling around Mount Kailas with Tsewang Tsambu (above), I was in Tibet again on another *National Geographic* assignment, 800 miles away from the mountain. We were accompanied by Chinese officials and had no Tibetan-to-Chinese translator. When we tried to find someone to help guide us to photograph the wildlife of the region, we were pointed toward an isolated nomad tent where the first person to emerge broke into a broad grin. By wild coincidence, I had run into Tsewang again, this time with his extended family. They invited us in and treated us like royalty. I made this photograph of his father and mother with other family members outside their yak-hair tent on a cloudy morning.

Nikon F3, 55mm lens, Fujichrome Professional 50

Nomad family receives blessings from photo of the Dalai Lama, Western Tibet; 1988

Before leaving Tsewang Tsambu's family (above) after two days of hospitality, I gave his father a photograph of the Dalai Lama. As he held it up to his forehead to receive a blessing in the privacy of his tent, I shot this photograph on a tripod. My Chinese jeep driver saw the old man emerge with the fresh Dalai

Lama picture in his hand. He told his superiors, and when I returned to the United States, I was notified that I had been tried *in absentia* in Beijing and found guilty of sedition. I wrote a carefully worded letter of self-criticism to the Chinese ambassador in Washington, D.C. This apology got the *National Geographic* off the hook so it could send other photographers to China and Tibet, but afterward I felt humiliated and ineffectual. As I mulled the situation over in my mind, I became intrigued by the implied power of that photograph of the Dalai Lama and how it was cleverly being used by the Chinese government to censor journalism in the United States about Tibet's true situation. Why did the Chinese feel so threatened? How could I tune into the positive power of that photo to make it work, not only for me, but also for the future of Tibet? Thus came the idea for *My Tibet,* a book of my photos with the Dalai Lama's words.

Nikon F3, 24mm lens, Fujichrome Professional 100

Tibetan nomad of Pekhu Tso, Western Tibet; 1988

While spending two days with Tsewang's family, my wife, Barbara, and I were invited to go on a wildlife search on Tibetan ponies. We sat astride wooden saddles covered with colorful saddle blankets—more secure, but far less comfortable than the bareback riding style of this nomad we passed as he was bringing a young foal back to a camp near ours. After I dismounted, I caught him with my camera and long telephoto lens braced on a pile of rocks.

Nikon F3, 400mm lens, Fujichrome Professional 100

Tibetan nomad riding below Kangbochen, Western Tibet; 1988

As I crossed a broad valley beneath this spectacular 7,000-meter (22,966-foot) peak, I spotted a horseman and waited for him to come closer. After I set my camera and telephoto lens on a tripod, he entered the already-composed photograph. I exposed for the snow peak because I knew it would be the dominant feature and that the rider would still stand out as a silhouette against the open plain. Grab shots of scenes like this rarely work because of the delicate balance of subjects and necessary depth of field to render them clearly.

Nikon F3, 180mm lens, Fujichrome Professional 100

Kiang (Tibetan wild ass), Paryang Valley, Western Tibet; 1987

Once a common sight in herds of hundreds, kiang are now confined to remote areas where Chinese soldiers can't shoot them from vehicles. Across open land, nonmotorized humans have no chance to catch these horse-sized wild asses once they begin to run. I recall spotting a group of kiang from a Toyota Land Cruiser going 35 miles per hour and driving toward their dust cloud for a full half hour at 15,000 feet without closing distance. They finally stopped to catch their breath, but veered abruptly into a gallup in a new direction as soon as we neared. I caught this group across a valley with a long telephoto lens while on foot.

Nikon F3, 400mm lens, Fujichrome Professional 100

Snow leopard (captive), Amdo Province, Tibet; 1981

I was able to make this image with a normal lens at very close range when I was allowed to come right up to the portable cage in which the leopard was being transported. It was absolutely calm and showed no aggression toward me. Although I've come very close to seeing snow leopards in the wild, as evidenced by fresh tracks and by sightings others made within minutes, I have yet to see one of these magnificent cats outside captivity. I'm not aware of any publishable photographs of truly wild snow leopards made without remote cameras or tranquilizer darts since my friend George Schaller photographed one in northern Pakistan with a long telephoto lens in the early seventies. The elusive snow leopard has become a symbol of the threatened wildness of the Himalaya, where they were never really common. They continue to range across the vast highlands of Asia from Russia and Afghanistan to Bhutan.

Nikon F3, 55mm lens, Kodachrome 64

Sunrise on Kangbochen from Pekhu Tso, Western Tibet; 1988

I made this image at sunrise with a wide-angle lens on the shore of the great lake, Pekhu Tso, where I camped for four days. I had gotten up before dawn to try to photograph black-necked cranes. Thus I was set up and ready when the first light struck these peaks near Shishapangma, the only 8,000-meter (26,247-foot) peak wholly in Tibet. The range was glowing pink under a cloudy sky that turned to snow flurries within a couple of hours. I used a gradu-

ated neutral-density filter to open up the reflection and hold the striking light on the peaks.

Nikon F3, 24mm lens, Fujichrome Professional 50

Rainbow over the Potala Palace, Lhasa, Tibet; 1981

This is my best-known image of Tibet. While spending time with Tibetans-in-exile in Dharamsala, India, I was often introduced as the man who took the rainbow over the Potala. None of them ever doubted that it was a straight photograph, but in the United States, many people assume it is computer generated, sandwiched, or somehow contrived. I didn't just happen on the scene. I was with a group of fifteen trekkers when I first saw a dim rainbow over a pasture to the left of the palace. The others accepted the scene as they saw it and took snapshots, while I visualized the rainbow appearing to emanate from the golden roofs of the palace and set out to make that happen. As I began to walk fast, the rainbow moved ever so slowly—too slowly—toward the palace. I ditched my bag in a bush and grabbed two rolls of film plus one camera and lens. Then I ran nearly a mile at 12,000 feet before the rainbow lined up with the image in my mind's eye.

Nikon F3, 75–150mm lens, Kodachrome 25

Women in the Jokhang Temple, Lhasa, Tibet; 1981

I had no idea what to expect when I entered this holiest of Lhasa's Buddhist shrines on a weekday morning in 1981. Hundreds of worshippers were waiting outside in line to prostrate themselves before great Buddhist effigies in the flickering light of yak-butter lamps. A few steps took me from modern Lhasa into the darkness of the Middle Ages, broken only by a dim glow of sunlight reflected from flagstones in a courtyard. But as this dim light bounced off the deep reds and golds of the Buddhist art that lined the inner walls, it made the pilgrims' faces glow with the warm, clear intensity of a Renaissance painting. Here I found a Tibetan counterpart to Rembrandt's *Nightwatch,* a vision to symbolize an entire culture. I singled out this family group of three generations with a short telephoto lens on my camera and tripod, taking multiple long exposures in hopes that one would not be blurred by subject motion. Only two worked.

Nikon F3, 85mm lens, Kodachrome 64

Pilgrims lining up to worship in the Jokhang Temple, Lhasa, Tibet; 1981

In the same Rembrandt light as in the above photograph, I made a wider-angle view of a group of worshippers in a brighter area of the temple. Despite the fact that Chinese Communist soldiers had stormed the Jokhang in the fifties, defaced its walls, destroyed its prayer wheels, defiled many of its images, and used the main hall as a barn for their animals, enough was left to draw pilgrims from all across Tibet. I recognized the dress of Khampas from the east, Goloks from the north, and Drokpa nomads from the far west. This image, too, was the result of many tries to get a several-second exposure in the dim light.

Nikon F3, 35mm lens, Kodachrome 64

Golok woman giving traditional greeting with her tongue, Amdo Province, Tibet; 1981

The Golok people were able to keep their traditions more intact than most other Tibetans because they forcibly resisted the Chinese invasion and were never fully subdued. In 1981, I found many of their mountain communes without a Chinese member or authority figure. Their religious practices, nomadic ways, and personal dignity were less altered than those of other groups I visited. Rumor had it that when Mao had sent in 6,000 troops to make good communists out of the Goloks in the fifties, 200 Chinese survivors escaped with their noses cut off flush with their faces. This young woman with a child was married to a wild-looking man who galloped through the hills with an AK-47 strapped to his side. She willingly posed for pictures, but acted momentarily unaware of the camera when she directed this warm greeting toward another approaching person.

Nikon F3, 85mm lens, Kodachrome 64

Yaks below Anye Machin, Amdo Province, Tibet; 1981

When Marco Polo returned from years on the Silk Road with his uncle in the late thirteenth century, no one believed his stories of giant cows with huge horns that gave milk. Seminomadic Golok Tibetans move across vast high pastures in spring and summer with herds of yaks that they raise for milk, leather, meat, wool, and dung to burn in their fires. These particular yaks were being used as pack animals for our expedition. I photographed them as they were being herded uphill toward our loads during a snow-storm. Otherwise, I would not have gotten an image of them all moving in the same direction like this. On a later journey into the wilds of western Tibet, I briefly saw a herd of much larger and blacker yaks, the wild ancestors of these semidomestic creatures.

Nikon F3, 35mm lens, Kodachrome 64

Russian-made airplane in ground fog, Chengdu, China; 1983

My 1983 American Everest West Expedition got up at four in the morning to board a charter flight from Chengdu to Lhasa. After several hours of waiting beside the fully loaded aircraft, the flight was cancelled when the heavy ground fog failed to clear. Before sunrise, I saw the potential for a great photograph with runway lights coming through the mist like a scene out of *Casablanca.* I put my camera at ground level on a tiny 4-ounce tripod and asked members of my team to stand in front of the bright lights to block flares getting into my pictures. The exposure was a full second on daylight film that gave the artificial lighting an amber cast similar to sunrise.

Nikon F3, 85mm lens, Kodachrome 64

View from the Lhasa Holiday Inn, Tibet; 1988

As seen from a high hotel window, Lhasa looks like any other medium-sized Chinese city. Taxis and tour buses are parked in the hotel lot, while across the road are grandiose Chinese buildings built in recent years. The monstrous Holiday Inn, with its 450 rooms, piped-in oxygen, in-house movies, massage service, and Tin Tin Bar is wholly out of character for the ancient, sacred city of Lhasa. The majority of foreign visitors to Tibet are based in this hotel and only experience the country for a day or two. After guided tours of old parts of the city, they fly directly back to China or Kathmandu.

Nikon F3, 20mm lens, Fujichrome Professional 50

Meadow below Muztagata, ancient Silk Road, Xinjiang, western China; 1986

Even though communism and tourism have impacted the traditional life of Kirghiz nomads who live near the Karakoram Highway, scenes like this one echo the writings of Marco Polo in the thirteenth century. The highway, which opened to the outside world in 1986, follows much of the ancient Silk Road that he traveled. He describes going through vast meadows at high altitudes set beneath two great snow peaks. Remembering his words, I used a telephoto lens to compress the hazy mountain in the distance and create the atmosphere of a vision out of the past with traditional Kirghiz life in the foreground. Six years earlier, I had made the third ascent of this 24,757-foot peak with two companions. We had used skis to climb up the mountain and to descend very quickly back into this world of meadows, flowers, and traditional ways of life.

Nikon F3, 180mm lens, Fujichrome Professional 50

Camel carrying skis to Muztagata, Xinjiang, western China; 1980

I made this incongruous photograph during a rest stop as the camel caravan of our 1980 expedition to Muztagata moved in timeless fashion across the Pamir steppes—with brand-new skis on their backs. Since each camel carried 220 pounds of food and equipment, rest stops were frequent. Being the first American expedition ever permitted to climb in the People's Republic of China, I had created a very different image in my mind of caravans of old. Our reality was a bizarre combination of buses, donkeys, camels, boxes, barrels, and skis coordinated by Chinese in uniforms carrying tape decks that blared out sounds like the screeching of an alley cat. The grating noise had emanated—several generations of tape copies before—as a pleasant melody from the throat of a Beijing soprano. I wrote in my diary that the net effect was that our expedition's approach to our mountain was taking on the sad, but distressingly funny, character of a fine show dog with tin cans tied to its tail. Only when we left our Chinese entourage behind at base camp did we truly experience the high and wild world of the Pamirs.

Nikon F3, 24mm lens, Kodachrome 64

Jan Reynolds skiing down Muztagata, Xinjiang, western China; 1986

I made this photo of Jan on the second day of our ski descent from 24,757 feet. On the previous evening, we had been on the summit together, but I did not get a dramatic close-up of Jan skiing there. As we neared our planned 8 P.M. turn-around time, the summit was not in sight and she was moving slowly with her boyfriend, Ned Gillette. With their permission, I took off ahead on the ever-more-gentle summit dome. I spent half an hour on top alone, taking a self-portrait with ice hanging from my face mask that appeared in *National Geographic*. Just as I was beginning my descent, they appeared and we skied down together, racing the sunset for 4,500 feet toward our high camp. At first we carved wide turns in perfect powder as the sun turned the snow to gold in light too dim to stop close action in a photograph. Then we plunged into the rising blue shadow of night to reach our tents perched beneath an ice cliff. The next day we carried heavy packs that made for poor downhill skiing and photography. Knowing we had no action close-ups, we stopped and skied this section without loads for the camera. At the time, Jan was the director of ski touring for the Trapp Family Lodge in Vermont, as well as a top national competitor in cross-country ski races.

Nikon F3, 85mm lens, Kodachrome 64

Kirghiz elder and son, revisited, Pamir Range, western China; 1986

When I first visited the Kirghiz area of the Pamir Range in 1980, I made the preceding portrait of an elder and son in a region closed to foreign visitors. In 1986, the opening of 16,000-foot Kunjerab Pass from Pakistan brought an influx of foreigners across this spur of the ancient Silk Road. My wife and I traveled by jeep over the pass and saw a few Kirghiz yurts spaced well back from the road as we neared the area of my old base camp of six years before. We stopped and walked over to the yurt pitched closest to the road, carrying a copy of my 1983 book, *Mountains of the Middle Kingdom*. Not speaking a word of their language, I wanted to show it as an example of my photography to help get permission to take their picture. As I opened the book to pictures of their area and turned the pages, a man grabbed it and ran off to another yurt. I was shocked and had no idea what was happening. Then he returned with the same elder and boy as in one of my pictures that he had seen. They were miles from where they had been camped with their herd when I took the earlier photograph. I gave them my copy of the book and drank fermented mare's milk with them before taking out my camera, yet again. The whole family posed holding up the old picture for comparison.

Nikon F3, 85mm lens, Fujichrome Professional 50

Kirghiz elder and son, Pamir Range, western China; 1981

As a member of the first American expedition ever permitted to climb in the People's Republic of China, I was able to enter a region closed to foreigners since the forties. While we set up our base camp for Muztagata in a meadow, Kirghiz herders emerged from their distant yurts to come watch the action. I spotted this man sitting on his haunches with his young son standing beside him. After coming up and greeting him, I began taking pictures of other scenes and he returned to intently observing our strange customs. I used a short telephoto lens to compose a sharp profile of his face juxtaposed in front of his son's face, out of focus in the distance. It took me more than ten shots to get the spacing and expressions just right, during which the old man never budged, even though he must have been aware that I was aiming my camera his way.

Nikon F3, 85mm lens, Kodachrome 64

Kirghiz horseman under Muztagata, Pamir Range, western China; 1980

The Kirghiz people are not only great horsemen, but also great show-offs. After this rider stopped at our camp, he departed along the crest of a ridge that profiled him against the mountain we were about to climb, while six of us shot away with our cameras. I sought to capture a decisive moment when the stride and attitude of the horse and rider would be in perfect balance with their setting. The horse's open mouth and forward stride work together to help symbolize these proud nomadic pastoralists who have resisted Communism, not only in western China, but also across the Russian border, less than 10 miles away.

Nikon F3, 180mm lens, Kodachrome 64

East Brigade Street, Kashgar, Xinjiang Province, China; 1980

I used a long telephoto lens to compress traffic on the main road out of this medieval walled town of Central Asia on a dusty summer evening. Situated at an oasis on the Silk Road beside the vast Taklamakan Desert, Kashgar is an ancient crossroads and trading center. I conceived of this photograph to set the stage for other cultural close-ups within the town itself. I stood on the road for a long time, to decide what moved me about the scene and how to put it all together in an image. I could hear the rustling of the Lombardy poplars that I wanted to use to lead the eye. I also wanted to find a camera position that would put Mao's statue facing out of the picture just above the trees, to help symbolize that he was on the way out of the picture. Other frames with cyclists and pedestrians in the foreground didn't work anywhere near as well as this one, where a single rider on a loaded burro symbolizes a timeless way of life that is still continuing after Mao.

Nikon F3, 400mm lens, Kodachrome 64

Uygur family harvesting wheat, Kashgar, Xinjiang Province, China; 1986

When I spotted this happy family working together to break the chaff from their wheat, I stopped to watch and photograph from a distance with a telephoto lens. I wanted to catch the father forking the stalks, as well as the donkey, mother, and boy circling the pile to stomp it down and separate the wheat kernels. After watching several circlings, I waited for just the right moment to capture the boy's joy with some separation between the other figures. More than 6 million Uygurs of Turkish descent live in Xinjiang Province. Before the Communist takeover in 1949, the region was called Turkestan.

Nikon F3, 180mm lens, Fujichrome Professional 100

Acacia tree at sunrise, Serengeti plains, Tanzania; 1982

When I got up an hour before dawn to see if I could photograph wildlife at a watering hole near our camp, I saw a faint red glow on the horizon. To my surprise, it became extremely intense about twenty minutes later, although it was confined to a tiny portion of the sky. Since I had a 600mm lens for wildlife, I used it to compose a landscape photograph in which the canopy of an acacia tree split the pink and blue portions of the sky. Other acacias in the distance added depth and a stronger sense of place to the image. My main problem was keeping my big lens steady enough for the half-minute exposure required at *f*32, the small aperture I chose to maintain depth of field between the trees at varying distances and the sky. I solved the problem by bracing the front of my lens on a rock with the camera body set on the tripod.

Nikon F3, 600mm lens, Kodachrome 64

Lions at play, Masai Mara, Kenya; 1982

While driving around in a Land Rover in the Masai Mara, we came across a pride of lions walking through tall grass. I focused my lens on them and began panning to follow them, even though they weren't out in the open or in quite the right light. When they reached a clearing, they suddenly burst into play that lasted about three seconds. The two lions in front turned about suddenly to pounce on the one in the rear. I caught the height of the action and expected something more to happen, but they instantly regained their regal poise and continued on as if nothing had happened.

Nikon F3, 400mm lens, Kodachrome 64

Lion cubs, Ngorongoro Crater, Tanzania; 1982

I spotted these cubs sprawled out on a granite *kopje* as their mother headed off toward a herd of zebra. We pulled over in our Land Rover and watched for a while, but the cubs staring into my camera seemed too cutesy an image for me. I wanted something that showed alert animals responding to the natural scene, not to my presence. After a few minutes, the cubs began to ignore us. When their mother finally returned, they all looked up expectantly away from the camera. In that moment, I got my shot.

Nikon F3, 400mm lens, Kodachrome 64

Buffalo skeleton, Ngorongoro Crater, Tanzania; 1982

The day before I made this photograph, I had watched a pride of lions devouring a freshly killed buffalo. When we came back at dawn, I expected to find the lions still feeding but a few vultures were the only live creatures we saw. They flew off the bare carcass only when we pulled within 10 feet of it so that I could prop a tripod on the door sill to photograph this stark scene. When we returned to Nairobi, we learned that a woman from California had been gored to death by a buffalo at the same time we were out in the field. Buffalo have been known to counterattack lions and kill them.

Nikon F3, 20mm lens, Kodachrome 64

Bull elephant, Samburu Game Reserve, Kenya; 1982

As we drove through the tall vegetation surrounding a water hole in the arid desert near Samburu, a bull elephant suddenly charged our vehicle. I got this shot with the telephoto on my camera by quickly bracing the camera on the roof through the observation hole in the top of the vehicle. Moments later, we were off and bouncing down the road. The elephant stopped its charge close enough to

reach out and touch our vehicle with its trunk.

Nikon F3, 200mm lens, Kodachrome 64

Hyena stalking flamingos, Ngorongoro Crater, Tanzania; 1982

Barbara and I saw more predators doing more things on the floor of Ngorongoro Crater than anywhere else in Africa. The crater has been called the world's greatest natural zoo, with the highest concentration of large terrestrial wildlife anywhere on earth. It is 2,000 feet deep, about 15 miles across, and, at the time of our visit, held about 9,000 resident large mammals. Cross-country driving was permitted then, so each morning we went on a game drive across the level floor, passing by a lake filled with flamingos. When I saw this hyena casually approaching the flamingos by looking unconcerned and wandering back and forth, I homed in on it with my longest lens and caught the animal against the birds just before they flew. The action of the birds flying did not make a better image because they were blurred in the low light before dawn and the hyena had ducked and turned away.

Nikon F3, 600mm lens, Kodachrome 64

Wild horses below Fitz Roy, Patagonia, Argentina; 1985

The sheer granite spires culminating in Fitz Roy (center) and Cerro Torre (left) are the most spectacular I have seen on earth. They lie in a small national park reached by a dirt road across the arid pampas from the little town of Calafate. No other visitors were in the park in October when we arrived to climb Fitz Roy very early in the season. Michael Graber and I had been out photographing the sunrise one rare clear morning when we spotted a group of wild horses. I set up my camera and framed the peaks with a broad foreground while Michael circled behind the horses out of view and came over a hill. The horses galloped full speed through my scene as I held down the motor-drive button and caught all their feet in the air only on this one frame.

Nikon F3, 85mm lens, Fujichrome Professional 100

Alpenglow in rain cloud, Patagonia, Argentina; 1985

I saw this unusual shaft of light in the clouds at sunset while I was driving a dirt road near Esquel that parallels the spine of the Andes. Instead of stopping right away, I kept on driving for

another couple of minutes until I could line up the strange pink shapes in the cloud with a mountain peak in shadow. A telephoto singled out just these features from a much broader landscape, profiled against a wedge of true blue sky. The red color in the snow is reflected from the cloud.

Nikon F3, 180mm lens, Kodachrome Professional 25

Stormy sunrise near Lago Viedma, Patagonia, Argentina; 1985

The clouds around the peaks of Patagonia are especially magnificent because they represent some of the world's most disturbed air. Winds generated off the Antarctic continent circle the globe almost uninterrupted by land in the latitudes of the Roaring Forties and Furious Fifties. The peaks of Patagonia cause the air masses to rise and create much wilder cloud patterns than elsewhere. On mornings when the sun rises beneath the cloud layer, vivid alpenglow becomes pink against the blue sky and snowy peaks. Here I was about 50 miles from Fitz Roy when the great light came. I purposely used a wide angle to take in a large part of the sky, quite unlike the concept of the above photograph.

Nikon F3, 20mm lens, Fujichrome Professional 50

Moreno Glacier advancing on beech forest, Patagonia, Argentina; 1985

What this photograph doesn't show is the large gap of water with floating icebergs between the trees and the glacier. The Moreno Glacier pours into giant Lago Argentina with such power that it completely cuts off a 40-mile arm of water. It then rises until its level is 60 feet higher than that of the main lake. At intervals of about three years, the ice dam bursts, creating one of the great recurring spectacles on earth. Thousands of tons of ice come crashing through the vortex in a continuous cataclysm that lasts for days until the water level equalizes. The lower half fills with giant icebergs, as if a part of Antarctica had been transplanted into the forested Andes. I made this photograph about a year after the ice had broken through. I decided to emphasize the strange juxtaposition of ice and forest rather than make the standard shot of calving icebergs that is so often seen in magazines and brochures.

Nikon F3, 85mm lens, Fujichrome Professional 50

Magellanic penguins, Peninsula Valdes, Patagonia, Argentina; 1985

 The region around this peninsula is one of the best places in the world to observe whales, elephant seals, and millions of penguins. I caught this freshly washed brigade just after they emerged from the sea on the way to their breeding colony in early November—the Patagonian spring. They had spent the winter in the Atlantic off the coast of Brazil. Here they echo the description of seventeenth-century British explorer Sir John Narborough, who saw them coming into the same colony "standing upright like little children in white aprons."

Nikon F3, 180mm lens, Fujichrome Professional 50

Guanacos at sunset, Patagonia, Argentina; 1985

 Although all my best close-ups of guanacos were made on the other side of the border in Chile's Torres del Paine National Park, this scene moments before sunset captures something more of the spirit of these wild relatives of the camel and the llama. The animals were not in a park and were definitely afraid of close approach. As soon as I spotted this herd profiled against the low sun, I put on my longest lens to catch the animals as they ran through the brightest part of the sun beam reflecting off the pampas. I wanted the scene to be absolutely simple, with no distracting objects or colors.

Nikon F3, 600mm lens, Fujichrome Professional 100

Alpenglow on Cuernos del Paine, Torres del Paine National Park, Patagonia, Chile; 1985

 I give this park the highest marks of any in the world for combined landscape and wildlife photography. For percentage of clear days, however, it gets the lowest marks. The peaks may not be visible for a week at a time, and a succession of storms can last much longer. Even during one of these bad periods, however, the appeal of the lower green hillsides dotted with wind-flagged trees and wild guanacos keeps any serious photographer shooting away. For me, the prime moments happen every few days at the first flush of dawn when, even in a bad weather period, the sun may momentarily drape the peaks in alpenglow. So it was on a windy morning that turned to rain minutes after I was waiting with my camera on a tripod near my tent pitched on the shore of Lago Pehoe. I made this image when

the peaks flushed pink, then used a wider lens to also shoot the cover photograph with a ten-second self-timer that allowed me to run into the frame.

Nikon F3, 180mm lens, Fujichrome Professional 50

Stormy sunrise through beech forest, Patagonia, Argentina; 1985

 I conceived this photograph by sitting down in the eerie beech forest surrounding our base camp for climbing Fitz Roy and trying to figure out how to visually communicate the feeling it gave me. On a sunny day, the shadows and branches became a complex jumble. On a day with fierce storm clouds overhead, sky patterns were too broken up by the forest canopy to come across as anything but grayness. Single trees against the sky could be beautiful, but didn't communicate the feeling of the thick forest. I finally imagined having the backdrop of a vivid sunrise and sought out a position in the forest to make a graphic silhouette with a short telephoto lens. I carefully chose the tree in the distance just left of center to be framed by two straight ones in the foreground at the camera position where a leaning tree would enter the frame in a long diagonal from the right.

Nikon F3, 85mm lens, Fujichrome Professional 50

Fitz Roy at dawn, Patagonia, Argentina; 1985

 I made this telephoto image during one of three attempts over a nine-day period to climb Fitz Roy. We would start in near-darkness in the forest and have this view as we came out on an exposed ridge at the level of the glaciers. Each time I made a number of photographs in the alpenglow, but on two occasions the weather failed to hold and we were chased down off the peak before we could start up the final 2,500-foot granite headwall. I brought along an extra-sharp 180mm lens to shoot portraits of the peak from this spot, then hid the lens in the rocks so I wouldn't have to take it up the peak. The extreme orange saturation is unfiltered, as indicated by the pure blue sky in the distance.

Nikon F3, 180mm lens, Fujichrome Professional 50

Cerro Torre from the summit of Fitz Roy, Patagonia, Argentina; 1985

 I never would have made this image if we had succeeded with our plan to climb the upper 2,500-foot face

of Fitz Roy in a day and rappel down to our camp in an ice cave. Icy rock in the early season slowed our progress, but we kept climbing because we felt we could survive a night out in the rare, clear weather we had been waiting for. We got past all the steep rock climbing and were on a short wall of firm ice that gradually broke back to the summit when darkness stopped us. After standing up all night without sleeping bags on a foot-wide ice ledge in 0 degrees Fahrenheit, we continued toward the top in murky predawn light. When the first rays of alpenglow hit Cerro Torre, I lay down in the snow and braced my telephoto lens to make this image. From the high vantage point it sets the alpenglow of transmitted warm rays on the peaks against deep blue snow in the shadows, where the scattered light is only reflecting the blue part of the sky. Many photographers complain that something must be wrong with their film or camera setting when they get blue snow like this, but the color occurs because of the light and location. That same objectionable blueness can be a treasured counterpoint of some of the richest warm colors on the planet recorded in the same split-second.

Nikon F3, 75–150mm lens, Fujichrome Professional 100

Michael Graber approaching the upper face of Fitz Roy, Patagonia, Argentina; 1985

 Our plan to climb Fitz Roy was to travel light and move fast in good weather. We hoped to climb the upper 2,500-foot face and get back to a bivouac in one long day. Here Michael is approaching the face as wisps of mist blow around it. Although we were only 200 yards from the cliff, the peak became veiled in clouds before we could get started rock climbing. As we beat a hasty retreat in high winds, the sharply etched snow ridge beside Michael was almost hidden from view by a ground blizzard. We descended all the way to base camp, waited out a storm, and made our successful climb days later. A much earlier start from our high bivouac allowed me to make a sunlit photograph of this spectacular spot.

Nikon F3, 35mm lens, Fujichrome Professional 50

David Wilson on the upper face of Fitz Roy, Patagonia, Argentina; 1985

 Toward the end of a very long day in which we were failing in our attempt to climb the upper face and rappel down again, I took out my camera and leaned over to catch David Wilson following up behind me. Although we still had more steep ice-covered rock above us, we had yet to discuss the inevitable fact that we were going to have to bivouac without sleeping bags on the upper face. We each came to terms with continuing on in our own way, aware that if we didn't want to go on, we needed to have spoken up. I found no excuses to give for going down: no clouds, no wind, no hints of moisture in the air. On this section we were already in the long shadow of the mountain. My fingers stuck to the cold metal of the carabiners and cam nuts that I was using for safety. This image captures that feeling for me, that sense of being way out there, yet exactly where we wanted to be: exploring one of the planet's grandest settings.

Nikon F3, 24mm lens, Fujichrome Professional 50

Michael Graber approaching the Italian Col on Fitz Roy, Patagonia, Argentina; 1985

As Michael Graber neared our intended bivouac site at the Italian Col, 6,000 feet above the base camp where we had started out that morning, I used a wide-angle lens handheld in just the right position to aim lens flares caused by the low sun at his figure. A minute later we crested the col together into high winds and saw a wall of cloud blowing in off the Patagonian Ice-cap. The extra rope we had coiled and carefully cached at the col a few days earlier was missing, blown away by winds that must have exceeded 150 miles per hour. Also gone was a food bag and a bottle of stove fuel. We turned around, rappelled down the ice gully, and found ourselves in the lee of the wind on a still night under a nearly full moon. Seventeen hours after we began, we returned to base camp in the forest to wait out the winds and try again.

Nikon F3, 24mm lens, Fujichrome Professional 50

David Wilson, Galen Rowell, and Michael Graber on the summit of Fitz Roy, Patagonia, Argentina; 1985

Reaching the summit of Fitz Roy minutes after dawn was our reward for a sleepless night near the top. We had spent the hours standing on an icy ledge, shuffling, wiggling toes, sometimes sitting briefly and shivering, sometimes running in place to get warm, watching our watches, waiting for the dawn. On top together, we watched the moon set over the Patagonian Ice-cap to the west as the sun came up over the arid pampas to the east. Then I set up my camera with a self-timer to make this portrait that captures the sense of joy that was bursting within us. As we stepped down from the summit, our thoughts turned to reaching a cramped snow cave at the base of the face beneath a boulder that now seemed like a palace that held all our worldly desires— warm sleeping bags, hot chocolate, freeze-dried beef stew, good company, and sleep.

Nikon F3, 35mm lens, Fujichrome Professional 50

Theater in Cleveland, Ohio; 1982

Every venue on a lecture tour is a different. I try to show up early to to get the feel of a place as well as to check out audiovisual considerations. When I arrived for a Sierra Club–sponsored multimedia slide show in Cleveland, I knew I had to record the scene for posterity. I pulled out a tiny Minox 35 from my briefcase and purposely underexposed this photograph to make the cheap backlit sign stand out from its surroundings. What the image says to me is that no matter how carefully a secondary visual input is prepared—a slide show, an exhibit, or a book, for example—one never fully controls the presentation of the final product, nor is it ever a true substitute for those primary, wild adventures where it all begins.

Minox 35GL, 40mm lens, Kodachrome 64

Editors

David Cohen, Collins Publishers

Erik Migdail, Sierra Club Books

Writers

J. Curtis Sanburn

Galen Rowell

Production

Janet Vail

Design

Mark Ong

Copy Editors

Amy Wheeler

Mark Rykoff

Our Thanks To:

Mountain Light Photography Staff

National Geographic Magazine

The New Lab

Sports Illustrated Magazine

World Wildlife Fund

Photography Credits

Page 5: Paul W. Hammond

Page 6, top: Lou Whittaker